THE REFERENCE SHELF (Contiued)

Volume 23

No.

2. Representative American Speeches:
1950-1951. A. C. Baird. $1.75.

No.

6. Gambling in America. H. L. Marx,
Jr. $1.75.

Volume 22

No. 3. Representative American Speeches:
1949-1950. A. C. Baird. $1.75.

Volume 21

No. 2. Representative American Speeches:
1948-1949 A. C. Baird. $1.75.

Volume 20

No.

5. Federal World Government. J. E.
Johnsen. $1.50.

No.

6. Federal Information Controls in
Peacetime. R. E. Summers.
$1.50.

Volume 19

No. 3. Free Medical Care. C. A. Peters. $1.25.

Volume 18

No.

3. Representative American Speeches:
1944-1945. A. C. Baird. $1.25.
5. Anatomy of Racial Intolerance.
G. B. de Huszar. $1.25.

No.

6. Palestine: Jewish Homeland? J. E.
Johnsen. $1.25.

Volume 17

No. 4. Representative American Speeches:
1943-1944. A. C. Baird. $1.25

Volume 16

No.

1. Representative American Speeches:
1941-1942. A. C. Baird. $1.25.

No.

6. Representative American Speeches:
1942-1943. A. C. Baird. $1.25.

THE REFERENCE SHELF

Vol. 28   No. 4

COMMUNITY PLANNING

Edited by
HERBERT L. MARX, Jr.

THE H. W. WILSON COMPANY
NEW YORK   1956

© 1956

By The H. W. Wilson Company

Printed in the United States of America

Library of Congress Catalog Card No. 56-7645

PREFACE

The editor of this volume lives in a small suburban community in northern New Jersey, close enough to New York City to be one of the metropolis' economic satellites, yet far enough removed to exist and flourish as a self-contained community with its own political, social, and cultural activities.

When the editor moved to this community (typically enough, from New York City) only a few years ago, there were many open or wooded spaces, giving to the area a genuine "country" atmosphere. Today, these spaces are largely "developed" into new homes or stores, or are already slated for early "improvement."

As the community grew, so did its many needs—economic, religious, social, cultural. Since 1952, two churches have been remodeled, one new one erected, and one is on the drawing board.

A large regional high school of sweeping modern design has risen on an abandoned race track site; a new grammar school opened last year—with "split" sessions from the first day; and the former high school is now a grammar school, renamed the "Village School" as perhaps a poignant reminder of the "old" days.

An eager group of citizens, mostly newcomers, has worked minor miracles to erect and equip a free public library—largely without the help of community funds. A small self-service grocery store has been remodeled to house a medical center; while at the other end of town a new supermarket rises on swampland.

Householders worry about their septic tanks, now no longer new, and wonder how soon the community can install a sewage disposal system—and what it will cost them in taxes.

And after most of this—not before—the town council activates a formerly inactive planning board, which in turn hires a firm of professional planning experts to draw up a master plan for the community. The master plan will take several years to prepare, and perhaps again as long to achieve official public acceptance. Then, after the town has neared its capacity for new development, it will have an organized program to plan its future growth.

This, in miniature, is the story of community planning in most areas of the United States. Every element is present: the rapid shift of population; the equally rapid springing up of institutions and enterprises to meet new needs; the ebullient, pioneering spirit of residents, particularly among the newcomers; and finally, an organized attempt to plan (largely after the fact) what the community requires for a healthy, satisfying existence.

This volume is devoted to a study of community planning in the United States today. Emphasis is placed on the positive means of achievement through democratically controlled planning, rather than on the many serious urban problems which require solution. One theme running through most of the selections is the opportunity and necessity for the individual citizen to participate in the planning process, to achieve benefits for himself and his family through working for the welfare of the entire community. By its nature, community planning is on the neighborhood level, much closer to home than many other municipal government undertakings. And as such, it is a challenge to every reader.

The editor is particularly indebted to the many organizations in the planning field which supplied copious suggestions. Acknowledgment is also gratefully made to the authors and publishers who granted permission to reprint materials, without whose cooperation these Reference Shelf volumes would not be possible.

HERBERT L. MARX, JR.

April 24, 1956

CONTENTS

VI. FEDERAL AND STATE ROLES IN PLANNING

VII. PUBLIC PARTICIPATION

I. PREVIEW OF PLANNING

THE TROUBLE WITH YOUR TOWN IS — [1]

What worries you about your town? The schools? The agony of fighting traffic? The exasperating lack of parking? The general decrepitude of the place?

Then you have a personal interest in these four brief stories of how other towns have found cures for similar complaints.

Town A, like yours, had a school shortage. Its school board planned a new building not far from the center of town. The site was in an area of creeping commercialism, but it was cheap, city-owned land.

Suddenly the school board was confronted with upsetting statistics. Most families around the proposed school were older folks, beyond child-bearing years. Before long, school kids would come only from other areas, places where not one house yet stood.

So the city traded its close-in land for $10,000 cash plus a building worth $75,000 that rented for $600 a month. It brought 40 acres farther out for $32,000, sold a strip of lots for nearly enough to recoup its investment and built the school there. The city got a better, more spacious school and came out ahead financially.

Town B, like yours, suffered from a congested downtown street. Irate citizens demanded that it be widened.

Investigation revealed that widening would cost $300,000. A traffic count proved that the jam was acute for only half an hour in the morning and another half hour in the evening. By resurfacing a parallel street, the problem was solved at half the cost of street widening.

Town C, like yours, had a parking problem. The usual remedies—new rules, meters, private lots, municipal garages— all were being advocated.

[1] Reprinted from *Changing Times*, the Kiplinger magazine. 9:21-4. September 1955. Reprinted by permission.

Then an air photo uncovered a better answer. It showed waste space inside nearly every downtown block. With the co-operation of merchants these spaces were cleared of shacks and refuse. Now Town C has plenty of places to park, off the street.

Town D's old fire hall was on a street so narrow that the trucks had to worm around parked cars before they could answer an alarm.

But the town did not build a new fire hall. It built a whole new civic center. The fire department got a better location, the city clerk got his first adequate office, the health department vacated its rented store, city employees stored city trucks in city garages instead of taking them home for the night, and the municipal electric power system got badly needed new quarters.

A few thousand dollars of appropriated funds and revenue bonds, to be paid off in twenty years from the power department's rentals, did the trick without financial strain.

In each case, you may have noticed, the obvious remedy was rejected for a less obvious but more practical solution.

Now, who would know where unborn school kids will live, how traffic patterns shift by the hour, how every plot of land in town is used, what the city needs to do its work well?

In each case, it was the same man, the city planner. He knew the facts and so could find the best solutions.

If you think of city planning as the speculative art of pro-ducing imaginary cities, as many people do, such hardheaded practicality may surprise you.

True, city planning is best known by such dramatic examples as Major L'Enfant's plan for Washington or Daniel Burnham's 1909 dream for Chicago, which has yet to be fully realized.

But today's city planning is different. Basically, it is a salvage operation. Planners take conditions as they are and attempt to guide future growth, to eliminate existing problems and to avoid foreseeable new ones.

Of 835 cities of 10,000 population or more, 716 have official agencies to do this kind of planning. Nearly a third of them are headed by full-time professional planners. In the rest, plan-ning is the responsibility of another official such as the city engineer, the city manager, the building inspector or the public works director.

Assisting them are groups of ordinary, nonexpert citizens like you who are members of local planning commissions. Some fifteen thousand to twenty thousand of these nonprofessionals are giving time and energy to work out their towns' futures, without pay.

They have no desire to create colorful plans that can be bound in stout covers and consigned to the archives. What they want is action, constructive action.

Their work begins with collecting four kinds of facts. First come physical facts: street layout, location of utility lines and boundaries, type and location of every structure, topographical features such as hills and streams. Next come population facts: how many people there are, where they live, where they work, their ages. Then come economic facts: how people earn their livings, how they spend their money. Finally there are facts about how people get around to shop, work and play.

Such facts, however, are not frozen. They shift like sands. So the planners look for clues to how land is being switched from one use to another, how population is growing, where people are moving and why, which industries are expanding, and which withering.

Many of these facts can be put down on maps and charts. Sometimes that is enough to spot a problem and point to its solution. The maps might reveal, for example, a haphazard lot-numbering system or show up interrupted streets that might be cut through to speed movement from residential areas to business districts.

The maps help the planners to mark out the town's future, too. They might indicate that the building of houses in one part of town should be discouraged because that area soon will be needed for new factories or warehouses. Or they might suggest that a section normally given to 25-foot lots be withheld for larger lots. Or they might suggest the need to save room for schools, playgrounds and broad streets.

From such decisions on how things ought to be, the planners put together another picture of the community, as it should take shape in the years ahead. The result is a "master plan," or "comprehensive plan."

But the final objective, you recall, is action. A plan is only an idea. It changes nothing until it is brought alive by such means as a zoning ordinance to control the use of land, subdivision regulations to assure that newly developed land will conform to desirable standards, and a capital budget program for constructing streets, parks and other public works that the city itself must provide.

This kind of planning affects everybody and is too important to leave to a hired expert or even to the handful of citizens the mayor appoints to the planning commission. The best planning comes when everybody pitches in, as did the citizens of Modesto, California.

This San Joaquin Valley town went through many years of standing still. Then during the war it began to grow, and by 1950 the population was 17,389. From 1951 to 1953 population increased almost 70 per cent, and the town's area grew by more than 60 per cent. Modesto was astonished to find itself expanding at the rate of four acres and ten families a day. In fifteen or twenty years it will be a community of 100,000.

Such pellmell growth was alarming. Modesto was in danger of losing all that had made it so livable and becoming just another crowded town, grown too large for its size.

Late in 1953 the city council appointed a Forward Modesto Committee, 53 local citizens representing a cross section of the community. Its job was to answer two questions: What kind of community do we want? What must we do to get it?

The committee split into sixteen study groups, each to consider a specific problem. Here are some of the problems and the first steps recommended to solve them.

Problem: Most major streets carry 15,000 cars daily. On Ninth Street, the main artery for through traffic, the volume is 30,000 a day. Within twenty years traffic will double.

Recommendation: Hire a competent traffic engineer, quick. Develop a master plan of land use and circulation by July 1956.

Problem: In five years the city spent $126,000 to maintain oiled, unpaved streets and only $88,000 on paved streets.

Recommendation: Require more durable streets in subdivisions and begin a ten-year street improvement program.

Problem: Not enough people ride buses.

Recommendation: Clean buses inside and out, publish schedules and review routes.

Problem: Despite long, hot summers Modesto has only two swimming pools, one at the high school, the other privately owned.

Recommendation: Let the city assist the schools in building one pool every two years for ten years.

Problem: In five years 27 persons drowned in irrigation canals.

Recommendation: Install floats below each crossing, handrails on both sides, steps wherever people swim.

Problem: City offices have only half the space they need. Also, the city has ten separate Federal offices, ten state offices.

Recommendation: Designate a civic center area where public buildings can be consolidated. Start plans for a new city hall now.

There were other problems, too, each with simple, planned solutions. The whole study was wrapped up in a report with an optimistic motto: "What gives our dreams their daring is that they can be realized."

Today Modesto has a purposeful plan for its future. It is an instructive example of what can happen when mere mortals put their hands to planning answers to problems.

If you belong to any group at all, service club, parent-teacher association, chamber of commerce, union, neighborhood association or whatever, you can have a share in planning your town's way out of its troubles. There are at least nine practical things that you might do:

If your town has no planning setup or only a partial one, you can agitate for establishing one that will work.

You can tell the official planners what kind of community you want to live in, thus aiding them to spot problems to be solved.

If you belong to a group with a special goal, be it eliminating slums or protecting songbirds, you can see that the group's cause is taken into account by the planners.

If you belong to a group with a special interest, such as a trade or a citizens' association, you can make sure that your interest gets all due consideration.

When specific chores need doing, perhaps conducting surveys or tabulating data, volunteer for duty.

When planning proposals are formulated, you can tell the public about them and explain their purposes.

If you favor the proposals, you can rally support for adopting them.

If you dislike them, you can criticize, organize opposition and see that your point of view gets a hearing.

Finally, you can help see that the planners get enough money to do a thorough job.

II. THE COMMUNITY'S NEED FOR PLANNING

EDITOR'S INTRODUCTION

Perhaps as a reflection of lack of foresight, most community planning activities in the United States have arisen as a result of critical problems demanding solution, rather than as a scientific means to avoid such complications and deficiencies. Before the planning process itself is examined, this section deals with a number of these problems which currently cry out for solution.

First, of course, is the fundamental growth and shift of urban population, dealt with in the first selection. We then turn to an intensive view of the world's largest, most crowded metropolis—New York City and its environs.

The next five selections each deal with a specific urban problem of today—presently as examples rather than as an all-inclusive treatment. Each discussion is presented particularly with a hopeful view of the remedies available or actually being effected. These are: (1) housing—and what can be done in an organized fashion to eradicate and prevent slums; (2) mass transportation—the changing roles played by public carriers; (3) the metamorphosis of "downtown"—its rise, fall, and possible regeneration; (4) parking and traffic—and some dramatic solutions to the dilemma of the automobile age; (5) public recreation—and what can be done despite conflicting pressures.

For two other important urban topics—schools and juvenile delinquency—the reader is referred to the Reference Shelf volumes entitled *Educational Opportunities for Youth,* edited by Walter M. Daniels, and *Juvenile Delinquency,* edited by Poyntz Tyler.

This section concludes with a review of the most recent and perhaps most perplexing addition to city planning headaches— that of defense against atomic attack.

OUR MUSHROOMING CITIES [1]

The landscape of America is changing. Cities are mushrooming out into the surrounding countryside. Rural communities outside the cities are rapidly becoming the suburbs of cities. These changes are creating new problems for city and suburb alike.

The pattern of cities with clusters of suburban towns around them is not new in America. Before the turn of the century, many people who worked in a city made their homes in a nearby small town. They commuted back and forth each day by railroad. They lived no farther from the railroad station than a horse and buggy or a street car could go in a short time. Thus suburban growth was limited to areas near railroads.

With the coming of the automobile and bus, that picture began to change. During the 1920's, many new homes were built in areas that were not near railroads. The owners of these homes could drive cars to the city or to a railroad that would take them into the city and to their jobs.

But the really large-scale moves to the suburbs began with the prosperity that has followed World War II—and it still is going strong. Millions of people have moved outside the border of cities to areas where new homes are available in large numbers at relatively low prices.

Many of these ex-city dwellers moved to towns that already existed. Others have moved into brand new communities such as Park Forest near Chicago, Levittown near New York City, or Lakewood in the Los Angeles area. In these new communities, thousands of homes stand on land that was meadow less than a decade ago. But most of the owners of these homes work in nearby cities.

One result of all this moving is this—it is no longer practical to talk about cities and outlying towns as separate units. The experts now speak of them as metropolitan areas or communities, meaning one or more cities and the suburbs that cluster around them and are dependent upon them.

[1] Reprinted from *Senior Scholastic.* 67:11-12. October 20, 1955. Reprinted from Scholastic Magazines by permission of the editors.

The Federal Bureau of the Census reports that in 1950 there were 168 of these metropolitan communities in the United States. And 84.5 million people—57 per cent of our population—lived in them. Almost one third of the American people lived in just 14 of these metropolitan communities in 1950. And the proportion has been growing constantly since then.

What has the change meant for the cities? The biggest problems arise from the fact that the cities are losing the most important group of taxpayers. The families who abandon the cities and move to the suburbs are not poor families. They are middle class families, each with an income of more than $4,000 per year.

It might seem that if the cities are losing population, they really don't need as much tax money, used to provide community services such as police and fire protection, sanitation, and street repair. But the fact is that cities need more of these services than ever before. The cities are still growing. Yet the money to pay for these community services is becoming harder to raise. The people who now move into cities generally have lower incomes than those who move out.

St. Louis provides an example of what this in and out movement means. During the period from 1940 to 1950, that city's population actually increased by 5 per cent. But almost all the families represented by that 5 per cent were very poor families. The average income of families living within the city's boundaries in 1949 was $2,718. But the average income of families living in the entire county (including the city and suburbs) was $3,628.

However, most cities cannot tax suburbanites to raise money for city street repair, police and fire protection, and other services which suburbanites use when they come into the city every day to work. As a result, many people who live in the suburbs and work in the city are getting services from the city for which they never pay a cent. The city, meanwhile, sees its former middle-class residential districts become slums. And the city doesn't have the money to clean, protect, or rebuild these slums.

Merchants who own downtown stores in the cities are watching their old customers move to outlying communities where they also do their shopping. In many areas, the owners of the

big downtown department stores have built branch stores in the
suburbs in the fight to get back some of this lost business. But
these merchants still have their main stores to operate, and they
need customers with money if they are to make a profit.

Many solutions for this problem have been proposed. Merchants complain that it is too difficult for shoppers to get downtown to shop because of the traffic congestion on the streets and
roads. In Pittsburgh, Atlanta, and several other cities, merchants
have formed organizations to work with city officials in finding
answers to these problems.

One answer is express highways—wide four- and six-lane
highways such as those being built in Detroit, Chicago, and Los
Angeles. But even if great numbers of automobiles can be
brought into the city, there's still another problem—where can
the cars be parked?

Some cities have established local government agencies to
finance and build large auto parking garages. In many cities
private enterprise has done the job. New types of garages
that automatically stack cars in special bins which take up little
space have been built in Washington, D.C., Harrisburg, Pennsylvania, Chicago, and elsewhere. In San Francisco and Pittsburgh, giant garages have been built under public parks.

But these efforts have not done a great deal to solve the
problem of city streets choked with traffic. Industry still is concentrated in large cities. So are many essential businesses. As
these enterprises expand, they bring more employees into the
cities from the suburbs. This chokes traffic even more than
before, especially with the tremendous increase in the use of
automobiles in recent years.

Two facts clearly show the traffic problem that plagues American cities: (1) There are only a fixed number of miles of
streets in a city, and that mileage has been pretty much the same
for years. (2) The number of automobiles in the United States
has grown from about 30 million in 1939 to almost 60 million
today. To solve the problem, then, we must either double the
number of streets (which can't be done), or increase the carrying
capacity of streets with still more expressways, garages and
improved traffic control and engineering devices.

However, with less income subject to taxation, and with a flood of new problems stemming from an influx of lower income families, the cities are turning to the Federal Government for more aid. In recent years, cities have been able to get direct Federal aid for express highways and other streets within their borders. And in 1949, Congress passed a housing law that granted $1 billion to cities to help them renew older areas that are turning into slums. This is a preventive measure, apart from Federal slum clearance aid, which helps pay for wrecking and rebuilding existing slums.

The suburbs are having growing pains of another variety. Experts say most of the problems of the suburbs stem from the fact that they are growing too fast. It is not unusual for a builder to erect and sell five hundred houses in a community in a year. That brings an entire schoolful of children into the suburb almost at the same time. Few communities have such school facilities available in advance. That means doubling up in classrooms.

The five hundred homes also need protection from fire and burglary. But few communities have the manpower or money ready to provide these services immediately. Of course they have all the new homes to tax. And the new money that comes into the community is plentiful enough to increase business for suburban merchants. But it often costs more to provide community services for a new home than that home will give to the town in new taxes.

Suburban communities don't have heavy industry which pays high taxes, and most of them don't want it. But bringing in industry does help the community's treasury, even if it doesn't add to the beauty. That's why some suburban residential towns are trying to bring light industry into their borders. Otherwise they must continually raise tax rates, as families have more children and require more community services.

A few large cities—in Pennsylvania, Ohio, Kentucky, and Missouri—have begun to tax the income of commuters who work within their boundaries but live outside them. This means that these people are paying taxes both where they live and where they work. Some economists think this type of double taxation will set the pattern for the future in city-suburb relations.

And city tax rates have been going up. In 1954, 481 cities with a population of more than 25,000 took a "tax bite" of $64 for every man, woman, and child in those cities. In 1953, city taxes were $61 per capita, and in 1952, only $56.

Tax rates in towns have been going up, too. People need more roads. They expect better schools for their children. And they want efficient government. In many small towns, officials have worked only part time in their local government jobs and held other jobs or owned businesses. Their official salaries were small. Now their public jobs have grown in importance and responsibility, and they must work full-time. So town government payrolls have been increasing.

Another pressing problem in many cities and towns is a growing shortage of water. In southwestern cities like Houston, Texas, the water shortage is already severe. There just isn't enough water in those areas. And big cities with heavy industry use most of the water, leaving little for outlying suburbs.

Some towns around Detroit have stopped all home building because of a shortage of water pumping equipment to supply new homes. Impure or inadequate water supplies can create serious health problems.

No one can say how the many financial, health, traffic, and other city-suburb problems will be solved. Probably there will be many answers. One that has succeeded in the past is annexation. This means that the city simply makes its suburbs part of the city. Many cities would like to do this in order to be able to tax their commuters. But the suburbs object. They don't want to pay the bills for city services. Besides, some state constitutions make annexation difficult or impossible.

Another possible solution is a super-government which taxes and provides certain services on an area-wide basis. Toronto, Canada, has such an arrangement. It covers the city and its suburbs. Water supply, sewers, mass public transit, health, and other facilities are handled jointly by officials of the city and suburbs working together in what is known as the Municipality of Metropolitan Toronto. [See "Toronto: Experiment in Federation" in Section IV, below.] It is a new idea in North America (though London, England, has had a similar arrangement for years). No one can say how it will finally work.

Nor can anyone really predict what the answers will be. One thing is certain: Neither the cities nor the countryside will ever be the same.

THE RUNAWAY CITY [2]

New York City is the extreme illustration of how the swirling growth of twentieth-century population, economics, and techniques has exposed our time-honored institutions of local government in metropolitan areas to a strain they cannot stand. Strikingly similar situations are to be found in our own country and abroad. Conceivably they can be met for a while by repeated postponement, patching up, and political makeshift; ultimately an enduring solution of the problem involving a recasting of the institutions of regional administration seems inevitable.

Historically, the City of New York was built around a port. The island of Manhattan was a great dock in a noble harbor. . . . Successive immigrant waves of Irish, Germans, and Italians landed there and stayed. Jewish migration after the Russian pogroms of fifty years ago, flight from a Europe torn by the First World War, an influx of Negroes from the South and Puerto Ricans from the Antilles, coupled with the unforeseen population increase of recent years, kept the city moving farther and farther beyond its historic lines.

The power of a metropolis kept drawing in people and activities that in turn multiplied both its attractions and its power. . . . The web of the city spread until it became the nucleus of ten per cent of the population of the United States. Still a port, the city was now a world financial center, a world transport center, and a market for American and foreign products of all kinds. Even more, it was the platform from which music, drama, art, fashion, books, and ideas of all sorts were launched and attained recognition.

[2] From "How Long Will New York Wait?" article by A. A. Berle, Jr., former Assistant Secretary of State and former New York City official. *Reporter.* 13:14-18. September 8, 1955. Reprinted by permission.

Increasingly city lines, city administrators, city economics, and city institutions lost much of their relevance. City Hall was more a badly organized management center for a huge set of public services of growing complexity than a government. Formally New York is a city governed from a beautiful Italian Renaissance building on the lower tip of Manhattan and from five branch offices—the five borough halls which have limited authority over local streets and public services. But half of the people in the metropolitan area are outside the city's jurisdiction anyway. Scarsdale, Jersey City, Hempstead, Summit, Mount Kisco, Montclair, and Massapequa are all in it. Their residents are working New Yorkers; but as residents and homemakers they have no responsibility and little relation to the metropolis. Basically New York lives upon, serves, and is served by sea traffic from the ends of the earth, by railroad traffic from north, south, and west; by automobile and truck traffic from everywhere, funneling into, shuttling through, and passing out of a complex which is at once market, sales office, banking medium, factory, school, and power center, whose life is drawn from an immense area.

The great depression of the 1930's forced the Roosevelt revolution, and the Federal Government picked up a group of unfilled functions that the states could not handle. It discharged them by creating a national system of planned finance, a national system of welfare, a national system of electric-power distribution, and the rudiments of a national system of stabilization of industry and agriculture. Washington occupied most of the no man's land between the states and the Federal Government.

But the cities? No one picked up the unfilled functions there. The struggle of the cities to survive, and of their adjacent regions to have services they needed, inevitably was intensified. The old city could not reestablish itself as a fully self-contained, self-ruling unit. Yet it had to go through the motions of administering itself as if it were one.

So it happens that in . . . 1955, out of its income base New York City's Welfare Department and charitable institutions must support its indigent and unfortunate to the tune of $222 million a year, in a time of peak prosperity, and each newcomer in New

York can claim a share immediately. New York City can get back a large part of this sum from state or Federal Government. But the city has no rebate or refund when it comes to paying the vastly expensive costs of medical care (the city hospitals alone cost $120 million a year), sanitation, and policing. The direct cost of relief to each working family of New York is estimated at a hundred dollars a year (before discounting state subsidies). In [nearby suburban] Westchester [County], relief averages out to less than five dollars a year per wage-earning family (likewise before discounting subsidies).

Government installations (of Federal, state, and independent Authorities) occupy some $1.3 billion worth of municipal real estate which the city cannot tax but must service. The 700,000 suburbanites as well as city dwellers who use New York's subways twice daily cost the city an average of seven cents each ride, since the city alone pays the enormous debt service on the transit installations and their fare covers only operating costs.

City revenues, like city boundaries and even forms of city government, are survivals from an earlier day. Modern taxation must relate less to "values" than to current productivity and income. National and state governments consequently finance themselves chiefly through income taxes of one form or another. When productivity grows, income and revenue rise, as do government expenditures. The surge of productivity in the United States has kept peacetime national and state income and expenditure in rough balance—almost, though not quite. Cities like New York, however, do not have unlimited tax powers and are debarred from a share of modern tax revenues.

They can levy real-estate taxes—and sales taxes too, if the state government authorizes; and they have a few other sources. New York has a combination income-and-sales tax in the form of a business gross-receipts tax, invented by the writer at Mayor LaGuardia's instance in 1934. But the city's chief revenue base is still ad valorem taxes on real estate and the essentially regressive sales tax. Both are economically limited. If sales taxes are increased, business goes somewhere else—that is one reason why "shopping centers" and department-store branches are mushrooming outside New York City now. Real-estate values

cannot go up more than just so much while there is rent control
—as there is in New York City. In consequence, the city with
a budget now of $1.75 billion (more than the budget of any
state government) must seek additional revenue. It needs, at a
rough estimate, three-quarters of a billion dollars of capital
funds merely to put its schools, hospitals, streets, transit, and
other facilities on a modern basis. Mexico City is more modernly
run today than New York.

New Institutions

Specific institutions had to emerge to bridge the historical
boundaries. They came.

The port of New York is a geographical expression paying
no respect at all to political boundaries. Part of it is in the
state of New Jersey, and the Hudson waterway carries ocean
traffic at least as far as Haverstraw. In 1921 a treaty was ratified
between the states of New York and New Jersey establishing the
Port of New York Authority, designed to coordinate policies so
that the port could operate more or less as a whole. The
Authority operates and collects tolls upon the Holland and
Lincoln tunnels and the George Washington Bridge crossing
the Hudson to the Jersey side; these are its great revenue-
producing facilities. It finances its operations by issuing bonds
secured by these and other revenues. Because trucks and buses
use these entrances, it created bus-line terminals. Because airline
terminals as such do not pay, the city turned over LaGuardia
and Idlewild airports to it. As it continues to take over functions remote from its original purpose, "Port of New York
Authority" is almost a misnomer.

A quite separate Authority—the Triborough Bridge and Tunnel Authority—operates other entrances into Manhattan under
the East River from the Long Island side. Since Long Island is
in the State of New York, a treaty was not necessary though a
state statute was. The Triborough Bridge, first despised by
bankers, financed itself by revenue bonds with the help of the
deceased Reconstruction Finance Corporation. It paid off. Presently the Queens Midtown Tunnel was turned over to it; still

later it built the great tunnel from the Battery to Brooklyn, giving truck access to Long Island. . . .

Schools had a somewhat similar history. Emerging from days when each village ran its own school, the New York City school system presently found itself involved in the growth of state-wide standards. New Yorkers, justifiably thinking that city government is always political, sometimes dishonest, and frequently inefficient, gave support to making education a New York State responsibility—and so it is. Eventually by statute the New York City school administration emerged as a kind of empire, connected with the city government only because its two boards—the Department of Education (which runs the lower schools) and the Board of Higher Education (which runs the municipal colleges and universities)—are appointed by the elected mayor. Standards are made by the state administration in Albany. No one believes (they are right) that the Board of Estimate or the City Council would be equipped to furnish educational standards and supervision.

The list of greater and less specific institutions, big and little, created to handle specific problems could be carried to interminable length. The New York Department of Water Supply delivers water to almost every faucet in the five boroughs; to do this it operates a four-hundred-mile system of aqueducts in Nassau County and through Westchester, Putnam, and Rockland counties all the way to the headwaters of the Delaware River. The Transit Authority, a separate entity, runs the subways. It will have to pick up the Hudson and Manhattan Transit tunnels to Jersey City and not inconceivably may inherit the Long Island Rail Road some day. And so forth.

So emerges the central problem: What is a "city government" today? Is there a "city"? What is "government" in these terms? What kind of institutions correspond to reality? . . .

Continuing invention of specific solutions for specific problems inevitably entails problems begotten by the solutions. Each new board, Authority, or government group rapidly becomes a center of power of its own. The Triborough Bridge Authority, for example, has the toll revenue from motor traffic coming from Long Island into Manhattan, from which it has accumulated

a tidy surplus of $18 million or so. (Meanwhile, of course, the
Long Island Rail Road, serving the same traffic, went into bankruptcy, from which it is barely emerging.) Robert Moses decided
that the city needed a Coliseum or convention hall—as indeed
it does—and Moses is a pragmatist who believes in doing what
you can do as and how you can do it. So the Triborough
Bridge Authority is developing Columbus Circle and lifting a
substantial area of Manhattan from depressing mediocrity into
twentieth-century functionalism. So also the Port Authority is
developing its tunnel head near Forty-second Street with bus
terminals; some day it may do the same thing for helicopters.
Whether the city needs a Coliseum or a bus terminal more than
it needs hospital facilities, or a bus terminal more than it needs
new schools, is a theoretical problem that remains unsolved;
the Authorities can do these jobs, and cannot build hospitals or
schools. The New York City Planning Commission, conceived
as a coordinator, has never developed power, and for practical
purposes can only contribute mildly toward coordination.

Short-changed by the state, without influence on the independent Authorities, without hope of substantial relief from the
Federal Government, New York, like other big American cities,
will probably jog along in this fashion for some years—until
there is an explosion. How the explosion will come is unfore-
seeable. Maybe because General Motors can make automobiles
faster than anyone can make roads, New York streets will be
choked to impassability. Perhaps because some major need is
left scandalously unfilled in spite of the congeries of Authorities.
Improbably because an atom bomb is dropped on New York.
More likely, the change will be forced by growing financial
strain. New public works and new services become increasingly
essential, but cities cannot indefinitely increase old taxes or float
additional bonds. More and better-paid teachers and more and
better policemen will be needed—are needed now; and more
services for health, for children and the aged. But revenues are
not available. Eventually national politics must legitimately
enter the situation when the crisis point arrives to make a solution
imperative.

Needed: a "New York Area Authority"

It is too much to hope that the existing and foreseeable strains will be met by long-range economic planning. Such planning in the case of New York would require joint action of the city government and the governments of the states of New York and New Jersey and, in the not too distant future, Connecticut, concurred in by the self-administrating Authorities. Even if all these agencies worked together, probably they could not act without some help from the Federal Government. Low-rent housing already is met by cities chiefly with Federal assistance. . . . It is hardly conceivable that Federal credit facilities will not be needed when the time comes. . . .

When the plight of our cities is faced up to at last, a fundamental attack on the whole problem of government in densely populated areas seems inescapable. Before this attack can take place, some basic ideas must be made clear. There are human values that can only be preserved by thinking in terms of small areas: the neighborly associations, homes and their qualities, contact between parents and schools. Even a New Yorker thinks not of the city or of his borough but of Gramercy Park or Brooklyn Heights, of West End Avenue or Kew Gardens, of his nearby school, his precinct police station, his familiar grocery. These are qualities of the village. For the rest, the city is a vast blur operated by political machines, a mayor—and other elected officials whose very names he hardly knows.

The actually powerful and functioning permanent officials, such as budget administrators, city and borough engineers, permanent administrators of housing, docks, hospitals, and finance, are almost wholly unknown. . . .

Analysis of the problem makes certain factors clear. Some economic functions have to be taken care of on an area basis: services and communications, water, transit, and main highways permitting entrance, exit, and access to the city and its parts, along with regulation of traffic and steady flow of supplies. These are as necessary to the suburbanite as to the inhabitant of Greenwich Village or Flushing. Nevertheless the centralized Authority, ramming its highways through, can wipe out the villages of human contact; the lively human centers even today fight a rear-guard action against the centralized blur that offers them services but destroys them at the same time. . . .

It follows, therefore, that somehow a system of government must be found that can do three things. It must liberate and protect the village for the things only a village can do. It must hold together the historical collectivity of the city for the things it can do. And it must set up some sort of entirely new overriding representative body to connect the sprawling population mass with its various parts and with the vaster population of outlying territory. In combination, the resulting system must operate intricate essential services, huge in scope, finance, and impact. It may not even be political in the old sense; its problems will be ninety per cent technical.

This is not theory. We shall, if the Twentieth Century Fund estimates are right, have a population of nearly 180 million by 1960 and perhaps 200 million by 1970. The New York complex, city and suburban, will be at least 20 million. In twenty-five years there is likely to be a continuous population mass from approximately New Haven straight down the Atlantic seaboard to Wilmington, Delaware, or perhaps still farther south. (The "New York area" is now almost a continuous settlement from Bridgeport to Trenton, with only a few shrinking unoccupied intervals.) The governmental structure built on historic townships, counties, and cities can carry the load only about so far. Eventually the whole problem must be met. . . .

The riddle is not insoluble. Two decades ago Franklin Roosevelt called into being the Tennessee Valley Authority to meet the regional problem of stagnation in the Tennessee Valley —which covered several states. He hung it on the peg of Federal government power over navigable waterways. Once organized, under the genius of David Lilienthal it invoked cooperation of the governments of several states and cities. The TVA built itself into a semi-autonomous regional institution that met a problem of regional underdevelopment.

New York, New Jersey, and Connecticut wrestle with the problem of overdevelopment, and there are many pegs on which they, with the Federal Government, could construct an institution. The Hudson and Long Island Sound are navigable waters; truck traffic is interstate commerce; the Holland and Lincoln tunnels are interstate thoroughfares; states have power to make treaties with Federal approval. There is government power enough to discharge the functions that are regional or national in character as distinct from those which concern only New York City, Jersey City, Hoboken, and the commuting towns. Federal financing should be available; have not Federal guarantees of mortgages and public-housing aid already rebuilt the eastern shore of Manhattan?

Village units within and without New York City could likewise be strengthened. . . . It should become a solid personal advantage to live within the jurisdiction of the "New York Area Authority" and at the same time be a resident of Morningside or Kew Gardens. . . .

We struggle today for order in the economic fabric, and the problem of the cities is not dissimilar. Functions still have to be apportioned. Centralized and representative institutions of technical capacity must necessarily deal with regional services. More localized institutions are still needed to deal with over-all area responsibilities. Tiny tenacious groupings are still needed to defend the hearth, home, and a modicum of beauty and esthetics. Political invention and construction must be accomplished in each case. The day of Authorities jerry-rigged to deal with a particular tunnel or development may be almost over. The riddle of twentieth-century area government is demanding solution. Cities like New York will not allow its solution to be postponed for long.

SLUM CLEARANCE PAYS EXTRA DIVIDENDS [3]

I have just completed a country-wide survey of the effects of the nation's drive against slums. I can report that it has boosted adjoining land values, improved business and raised tax receipts. It is also saving taxpayers millions of dollars in reduced police and fire-protection expenditures, and welfare and hospital costs.

[3] By Donald Robinson, free-lance writer. *Reader's Digest*. 67:87-90. November 1955. Copyright 1955 by The Reader's Digest Association, Inc. Reprinted with permission.

As President Eisenhower has remarked, "It is good business to fight slums."

The slum problem is enormous: according to the United States Public Housing Administration, 7 million of our 45 million dwellings are close to being unfit for human beings to live in, by American standards. Millions of others are rapidly approaching that state. Federal records show that our slums are directly involved in 45 per cent of major crimes, 55 per cent of juvenile delinquency, 60 per cent of tuberculosis cases, 50 per cent of all diseases, and 35 per cent of fires.

The very existence of slums entails heavy financial penalties to a city. The slums of Atlanta, Georgia, were at last count consuming 53 per cent of all city services while paying only 6 per cent of the real-estate tax. In Baltimore every acre of slums was producing a deficit of $2500 a year for the municipal government.

Two years ago New York City officials decided to learn what financial effect a slum-clearance project has on the area surrounding it. They studied the thirty square blocks around the Red Hook public-housing project in Brooklyn where its influence could be directly felt in terms of trade and commerce. They found that the total assessed valuation of the buildings in this area had gone up 50 per cent in the five years since the site was acquired, while property values in Brooklyn as a whole rose only 23 per cent.

A private slum-clearance project in Manhattan—Stuyvesant Town, erected by the Metropolitan Life Insurance Company during 1945-1949—did even better. Assessed valuations on the thirty-two-block area bordering Stuyvesant Town had in 1953 increased 68 per cent since the site was acquired. On one three-block stretch on Fourteenth Street, they were up 192 per cent.

And look at Pittsburgh. A drive was launched in 1949 to rehabilitate sixty slum acres. The state ripped down every building in half the area and made a park, while the Urban Redevelopment Authority built a housing project on the remaining land. By the beginning of this year, despite the fact that thirty acres had been taken off the tax rolls, land values alone in that rehabilitated district had soared $10.5 million. Leslie J. Reese, director of the Pennsylvania Economy League, says, "The redevelopment program has affected the entire city, and it is estimated that the over-all gain during the first five years was $35 million in valuation."

These jumps in land values are a bonanza for hard-pressed city governments. It is estimated that New York is making more than two million dollars in extra taxes from land whose worth has been boosted because it adjoins the city's thirty-three slum-clearance projects. Murfreesboro, Tennessee (population 13,000), used to collect $2000 a year in taxes on its slum areas. Today, after an intensive campaign to rehabilitate slum buildings, it expects to collect $20,000 from the same areas. In Perth Amboy, New Jersey (population 41,000), it is estimated that redevelopment of slum areas will increase tax receipts from $23,621 to more than $170,000.

The public-housing projects themselves usually pay into the city coffers 10 per cent of the rentals taken in. At last report Memphis was getting $95,444 in such payments from seven public-housing projects. If the slum buildings that were replaced were still standing, their tax payments would be only $35,649.

The attack on slums is three-pronged. First and biggest is the public-housing program under which the Federal Government (plus a few state governments) has been helping cities to raze slums and erect low-rent housing for needy families. Since 1935 nearly 2000 undertakings have been completed which provide room for almost two million people. Units now, or soon to be, under construction will house 150,000 more.

Second is rehousing by private enterprise. Life insurance companies and other firms have cleared slum areas and constructed housing for hundreds of thousands of people.

Third is urban rehabilitation, one of the measures in the nation-wide citizens' campaign sparked by ACTION, the American Council To Improve Our Neighborhoods. [See "ACTION for Your Community" in Section VII, below.] Through more rigid enforcement of housing codes and the voluntary cooperation of landlords, slum sections have been renovated in scores of cities. More than 110,000 buildings have been salvaged since January 1, 1952.

The fight on slums has had tangible effects in the health field. Dr. Jay Rumney, professor of sociology at the University of Newark, New Jersey, made a two-year study comparing the health records of tenants in three Newark public-housing projects with those of people living in three slum areas—the same sort from which the majority of the public-housing tenants had come. Dr. Rumney found that, in the fifteen-to forty-year-old age groups, the number of new cases of tuberculosis was 6 per 1000 people in the slums—and 3.3 in the housing projects. There were 40.6 infant deaths per 1000 births in the slums, only 34.7 in the projects. Among children under fifteen the incidence of communicable diseases—whooping cough, measles, scarlet fever, chicken pox, mumps and German measles—ran 163.5 per 1000 in the slums, 114.2 in the projects.

Dr. Rumney's findings prove that Newark taxpayers save thousands of dollars a year on ambulance runs, visiting-nurse calls, and hospital care. A Newark ambulance driver, talking about one slum area now replaced by public housing, was explicit: "I'd hate to count all the last-ditch TB cases I used to move out of that district. Now I don't see a bad case for months at a time."

Baltimore's rehabilitation plan is reported to have been a factor in a 45 per cent drop in the tuberculosis death rate; in Miami the Health Department noted a 50 per cent drop.

The fight on slums has had impressive, concrete effects on juvenile delinquency. In Cleveland the delinquency rate among 4018 boys and girls in six housing projects averaged only 1.57 per cent, whereas in adjoining slum areas the rate was 2.26 per cent. In Philadelphia the rate of juvenile arrests in fifteen projects was 2.1 per cent, but in the slum areas—where most of the public-housing children lived formerly—the rate ranged as high as 11.6 per cent.

One reason for the lower delinquency rate in the housing projects is the better home life afforded. A second is that many projects provide clubs and recreational facilities for youngsters. A third is that most project managers won't tolerate serious misconduct by tenants' children.

Last year a gang in a Savannah, Georgia, project tried to set fire to one of the buildings. The parents wailed, "We just can't control our children."

The manager was adamant. "Make your kids behave or out you go." Overnight the children began to toe the line.

Dr. Rumney, comparing school records of 93 Newark slum children before and after they had been rehoused, found they had improved 7 per cent in attendance, 10 per cent in academic grades, 16 per cent in personality-development grades and 19 per cent in health-habit grades.

Yamacraw Village, formerly one of Savannah's most notorious sections, shows the impact of slum clearance on crime. According to the city's police department, before Yamacraw Village was built 19 per cent of Savannah's crime originated there. Now less than 1 per cent.

Elsewhere the story is the same. "Those housing projects are running us out of business," a desk sergeant in Norfolk, Virginia, Second Precinct recently said. In Baltimore a detective told me: "I know one place where it wasn't safe for a man to walk even in the daytime—you were practically sure to be mugged. Now even women can go out alone at night. All the hoodlums have moved away. 'Hoods' are like rats. They hate to live in a decent environment."

Better housing has materially reduced fire costs. In Newark Dr. Rumney found that there were nearly four times as many fires in slums as in public-housing projects. He estimated that the cost of fire protection was $1,115 per 1000 dwellings in the slums, whereas for public housing it is only $295.

A more important saving is in human lives. Last year a majority of the 133 New Yorkers who were burned to death were living in slums. But not one life has been lost to fire in New York City's public housing. Similarly with fatal home accidents, which numbered 25 per 10,000 persons in the slums against none in the housing projects.

It is sometimes charged that slum dwellers are incapable of appreciating better homes: "They turn them into pigsties." Actually most tenants of housing projects are so proud of their apartments they keep them spotless. The New York City

Housing Authority evicted less than 200 of its 74,459 lease-holders last year for failure to care for their apartments.

One more by-product of the fight on slums is noteworthy. A study in North Carolina several years ago revealed that a third of the 194 white families and half of the 112 Negro families who left public-housing developments moved into their own homes. A sampling in Louisville showed that 414 of 764 families who moved from low-rent projects between 1940 and 1950 bought homes.

"Public housing creates hope," says Charles E. Slusser, head of the Public Housing Administration, "and hope for the future is the fuel that powers the engines of private enterprise."

MASS TRANSPORTATION [4]

Historians of the future will certainly record December 1, 1952, as the day when a major American metropolis first publicly acknowledged that its transit system rated a break instead of a knock. That was the day when conservative Philadelphia prohibited all curb parking in the 112 blocks comprising the heart of the city's shopping and business district.

The ban, involving the cancellation of an established privilege, was even more remarkable because the suggestion came from the city's transit utility—which, like transit companies in many American communities, long had been a public whipping boy. . . .

The Philadelphia Transportation Company, however, faced a desperate traffic situation. The congestion in the downtown district threatened to paralyze all movement of autos, trucks, and transit vehicles in the three shopping weeks before Christmas.

"If utter chaos is to be avoided . . . drastic remedial measures must be taken," R. F. Tyson, PTC executive vice president, warned the mayor.

Furthermore the PTC notified the newspapers of its warning and its proposed remedy.

[4] From "Mass Transportation or Mess," article by Sam Stavisky, free-lance writer. *Nation's Business*. 41:32-3. June 1953. Reprinted by permission.

Ordinarily, the PTC plan would have done little more than inspire a stream of derisive letters to the editor. But, among the first to learn of the suggestion was youthful, dynamic Robert K. Sawyer, Philadelphia's city managing director. He read the papers on his way to work and, by the time he reached City Hall, had determined on action rather than debate. Backed by Mayor Joseph S. Clark, Jr., the city manager ordered the curb parking ban put into effect as a pre-Christmas emergency traffic measure.

The experiment was an instantaneous success. . . .

Having seen how smoothly traffic could flow through the downtown streets, the city heads extended the ban for three months, then took steps to make it permanent by city ordinance.

Philadelphia benefited in a number of ways. Traffic accidents were reduced by 20 per cent; the flow of autos and trucks was speeded up 27 per cent; the passage of fire engines was expedited; cab rates, geared to time as well as distance, were lowered, while the drivers' daily take in trips and tips was increased.

But the most dramatic daily effect of the ban was the substantial improvement of bus and streetcar service in the business district. The transit vehicles moved faster, delays were reduced, and the frustrating cutback—when the operator gives up trying to complete his run and pushes out his passengers with advice to board the next approaching vehicle—was cut by 50 per cent. New Jersey residents commuting to Philadelphia by bus save 20 to 25 minutes per round trip. . . .

And how was downtown business affected by the parking ban?

The merchants—with few exceptions—discovered their business depended not on the number of vehicles but on the number of people who came into the central city. Although some specialty shop merchants still feel that the parking restriction scares off one-stop shoppers, the Philadelphia Merchants Association, originally cold to the idea, found—in the words of a spokesman—that it did a "world of good." . . .

Most significant angle of the Philadelphia story is not in its immediate traffic and transit relief, but in its long-range impact.

Philadelphia is beginning to realize—as most cities eventually must—that its transit system is the lifeline to its downtown shopping and business center.

Even before the ban, some Philadelphia civic leaders and businessmen were aware of a survey which showed that approximately 85 out of 100 shoppers in central city arrived there by transit, as against 9 out of 100 by auto. (The survey also showed that autos parked at the curb represented only 2.2 per cent of the downtown shoppers.)

Thus, in improving its transit service, Philadelphia improved and strengthened its lifeline at a time when the nation's cities are threatened with loss of trade, lowering of commercial property values, and reduction in tax revenues as a result of the postwar boom in automobile ownership, traffic congestion, and the migration of large segments of the city population into the suburbs.

The situation in Philadelphia is symptomatic of the primary problem which many cities face. Surveys have disclosed that 75 out of 100 central city shoppers in Atlanta come via transit; 81 out of 100 in Indianapolis; 65 out of 100 in San Francisco. "Sixty to 80 per cent of the working people and shoppers depend on transit in our larger cities," reports the Transportation Department of the Chamber of Commerce of the United States. Philadelphia has shown other municipalities whose central core is menaced by decentralization one simple, inexpensive way to help stem the trend. Already a score of communities have sent experts and observers to Philadelphia to see for themselves the effects of the tradition-breaking experiment.

The curb parking ban—it must be emphasized—is but one treatment, and not a cure for either the transit or traffic crises. Nonetheless, the Philadelphia story represents a genuine gesture by local government to ease not only the traffic jam but to assist its transit system, at a time when most municipalities are still feuding with their own transit utilities over rates, rights, fares, taxes, and the like.

The ironic fact is that the cities and the transit systems are both suffering from the same disease and should be working together to find a cure.

In 1940, some 32 million motor vehicles were registered in the United States, and the cities already were groaning that their streets were unable to handle the traffic congestion.

In 1952, a total of 53 million autos and trucks were jamming streets and highways. By 1969 according to the Department of Commerce estimates our roads will be clogged with 100 million vehicles.

The widespread ownership of autos stimulated the movement of city folks into the surrounding countryside; and at the same time, the steadily worsening central city traffic congestion discouraged the suburbanites from coming downtown, accelerated the rise of suburban shopping centers, further attracting city dwellers into the suburbs. The resulting loss of customers by the central city business core has deteriorated downtown property values, thereby cutting municipal tax revenues. . . .

Meanwhile, the transit industry has been victim of a similar vicious circle. As motor vehicle registration has mounted, passenger volume on streetcars and buses has declined, from a wartime high of 23 billion riders in 1946 to 15 billion in 1952; the prewar passenger level in 1941 was 14 billion. Thus, while the nation's population increased by more than 10 million, transit traffic increased in eleven years by only 1 billion.

The loss of passengers, together with the inflationary postwar increase in the cost of labor and materials, forced the transit companies to raise fares. Each rate increase—as many as seven on some systems since the end of World War II—in turn reduced the number of passengers. At the same time, the spread of population to the suburbs created pressure for the companies to extend their bus runs into comparatively sparsely settled areas where passenger volume was insufficient to pay for the cost of servicing the routes.

As a result, since 1945 the transit industry has had rough riding. Few of the 1,641 operating companies can report a "fair profit." . . .

Loss of passengers is the chief cause of the transit industry's decline. Attempts to replace streetcars with more flexible buses, with more comfortable vehicles, with other improvements in service, have been inadequate to cope with the strangulating

effect of traffic congestion. In San Francisco, for example, the
Municipal Railway tore up its trolley tracks on one route, re-
paved the street, and put on new buses to attract riders. The
move proved to be profitless, because the improved thoroughfare
also attracted more autos and created a bigger traffic jam.

Besides the increasing competition from the auto, however,
the transit industry also has been hurt by the general application
of the five-day work week, seriously reducing Saturday transit
business. Sunday always was a poor day. . . .

While suffering from a 35 per cent decline in passengers,
the transit industry since V-J Day has been painfully experiencing a steady rise in the cost of doing business—not unlike other
industries. The cost of transit labor has shot up more than 100
per cent in some cities and the cost of labor represents more
than 65 per cent of the transit industry's annual operating expenditure. Cost of replacement vehicles and fuel have also risen
sharply.

Unlike most other industries, however, the transit utilities
have not been able to catch up with their increased costs. . . .
In some cities, the cash fare has zoomed to twenty cents—Chicago,
Detroit, St. Louis, Minneapolis, Cincinnati, Seattle, and Kansas
City. . . . But there's a practical limit to increasing fares because
each boost squeezes out a percentage of riders, who walk, take
to their own autos, or form car pools. . . .

The Hatfield-McCoy relationship between many local governments and their transit utilities repeats itself in their annual
arguments over taxes. The transit industry complains it is
soaked by excessive taxes for reasons no longer existing and, in
some cases, long since forgotten. Most irksome of these levies,
in the eyes of the industry, is the "outrageous" and "confisca-
tory" gross receipts or franchise tax.

The city fathers—and sometimes state authorities as well—
slapped the 1 to 5 per cent gross receipts tax on the transit
utilities back in the pre-automobile "good old days" when the
car lines held a tight monopoly on mass transportation. It was a
special tax levied for the use of city streets and for the privilege
of doing business. . . .

There are other "soak-the-transit" taxes that rankle the industry, taxes which, since the end of World War II, have spelled in many areas the difference between profit and loss. Some cities tax their local transit companies to maintain, or help support, the traffic police, public parks, street cleaning, street sprinkling, snow removal, street lighting, bridge construction, etc. These levies are in addition to the regular Federal, state, and local taxes carried by any business firm. . . .

The transit men also insist there's no longer any valid reason for a utility to subsidize public education through cut-rate fares, any more than grocers should cut the price of milk or bread or meat for school kids. In Washington, D.C., for instance, school children pay a three-cent fare, as against a normal cash fare of seventeen cents.

Some suggest that the way to deal with transit problems is to turn them over to public ownership and operation. Today there are 39 publicly owned transit systems, but these, despite tax rebates and other benefits, aren't doing any better than the privately operated lines, in terms of fare or service.

Political interference undercuts efficient management of some municipally operated lines. Losses on public transit systems must be paid for somehow—and the losses may be high. In Boston the Metropolitan Transit Authority lost $5,315,000 in 1951—a sum that had to be made up through higher real estate taxes in the city and 13 neighboring communities. Detroit's municipal system lost $3,681,000; New York's city-run lines dropped $100 million in fiscal 1951-1952.

The headaches of public ownership are today well enough understood so that few municipalities approach the prospect with eagerness. The trend, if anything, is away from public ownership.

Not public ownership, but public understanding, is the approach to solving the problem.

In the future, say the planners, some communities will set aside streets for the exclusive movement of buses. Sidney H. Bingham, chairman of the New York City Board of Transportation, even foresees the day when all pleasure cars may be barred from the city's central core.

Once the public authorities recognize the vital importance of a healthy mass transit system, they will take steps—as Massachusetts has—to speed up the regulating process so that fares can be raised to meet increased costs without an unreasonable lag. More equitable methods also will be worked out to give the transit utility a fair chance to earn a fair return, so as to encourage private investment in the lines. As to the tax load, some communities—mainly to meet strike or shutdown situations—already have shown the way by reducing or eliminating the hated gross receipts tax, and other direct and indirect imposts.

The transit industry itself, long sulking with a nobody-loves-me complex, has in the past couple of years come out of its corner and publicly proposed—as in Philadelphia—new ideas to help itself and its community.

Some lines have come up with reduced fares for family rides, for shopping days, for special night events, etc., to stimulate transit business. Some companies have installed newer, bigger, more comfortable buses and trolley coaches. Some utilities have tried zone fares, instead of flat fares, to encourage short-haul rides. Some have launched intensive local publicity campaigns to change public derision into understanding.

Roger W. Babson, the investment counselor, sees the day in the near future when city government will go all out to help the mass transit systems, and to urge public use of buses and streetcars as a matter of municipal self-survival. He envisions the day when transit companies will exploit other sources of revenue, such as transit ads, transit radio, silent movies, and even commercial spot announcements by the bus drivers: "Next stop Thirteenth Street. The Boston Store is having a special sale of white goods." The financially haggard transit companies of today will prove tomorrow to be a "gold mine," Mr. Babson predicts.

Meanwhile, for the present, the increasing traffic congestion and flight to the suburbs make it increasingly clear that it's up to the municipalities to help themselves by helping improve and strengthen their transit lifeline.

"DOWNTOWN" AREAS [5]

United States merchants are going back downtown to do the biggest planning job in their history. They must revitalize the central cities, which have decayed at the core while the suburbs have been growing and flourishing.

Their interest is understandable. ⌈If something isn't done about the problems of the city, downtown merchants stand to lose not only a lot of customers but also a considerable real estate investment.⌋ And the situation in many cases is becoming critical.

The classic case among United States cities is sprawling Los Angeles. Back in 1919, the downtown area did 74 per cent of the retail business of Los Angeles County. In 1950, the figure was 35 per cent; in 1954, 29 per cent. Dallas is another exhibit. The latest Bureau of Census figures show that retail sales in downtown Dallas over the 1947-1953 period stayed at $170 million, while total retail sales for the metropolitan area rose from $226 million to $837 million.

The scope of the job was made clear . . . by a [recent] statement by Philip M. Talbott, . . . president of the National Retail Dry Goods Association . . . [who] announced a new major program. NRDGA's chief target, . . . he said, will be the rehabilitation of downtown areas.

"This effort involves a frontal attack," said Talbott, "on the problems of rapid mass transportation facilities, slum clearance, parking, and the many other facets that enter into urban life."

It is clear that retailers have learned to look well beyond the curb in front of the stores. . . . NRDGA . . . [has] released the results of a nation-wide sampling of its membership, the purpose of which was to find out what are the major problems and what, if anything, is being done about them. The replies show not only that there is an intense interest in the problem throughout the country, but also that much activity has been generated by it. Here are some of the current projects:

[5] From "Retailers' Problem: Reviving a Sick Old 'Downtown,'" article. *Business Week*. p42-4. January 15, 1955. Reprinted by permission.

Flint, Michigan, is developing a one-way street system to speed traffic through the downtown area. Denver voters have approved a $4 million bond issue to create off-street parking facilities. Danville, Illinois, businessmen have subscribed $125,000 to a parking corporation. Stockton, California, provides free bus transportation downtown for shoppers on sale days. New Kensington, Pennsylvania, is launching a face-lifting program for the downtown business district.

And so it goes. City after city across the country is making a stab at curing the ills that plague it. There are some very ambitious plans under way, several of which have already received considerable publicity. For instance; Pittsburgh's re-doing of the Golden Triangle area; Philadelphia's ambitious plans for the "Chinese Wall" of the Pennsylvania Railroad that used to divide the town; Boston's proposed big Back Bay center for business, pleasure, and shopping. There are elaborate programs of slum clearance and civic improvement going on in Baltimore, St. Louis, Chicago, and Indianapolis to name four cities in which merchants have played a big role.

Many of these projects have been spurred by Title I of the Housing Act of 1949, which offers Federal aid in clearing blighted areas for redevelopment. A 1954 liberalization of the act is expected to spur urban redevelopment even further. [See "Urban Renewal Under the Housing Act of 1954," in Section VI, below.] There are in all an estimated 1,000 redevelopment authorities in the country today, mostly at municipal level.

The Houston Example

Although a number of these plans are comprehensive in nature, there is a big question whether many of the programs under way are sufficient to deal with the evils involved. Piecemeal reforms sometimes can do no good at all. In some cases, they even help to increase the evils they are meant to cure.

Houston provides an interesting example of how partial planning can let things drift further out of whack. A few years ago Houston started a determined effort to build itself a number of parking garages. The results have been impressive—6,732 places for cars already, and more spaces a-building.

But observers feel that Houston is still desperately short of parking spaces. Auto registrations in Harris County went from about 200,000 in 1947 to 400,000 last year. Observers wonder, too, what is going to happen a few years from now when an ambitious program of speedways will be finished, funneling still more cars downtown.

Meanwhile, something else has been happening. In 1947, the public bus system carried 106 million passengers. Last year it carried about 65 million—indicating a huge increase in car traffic into the city. Out of this experience has come a new thought for the bustling Texas city. Says an observer: "One answer appears to be fringe parking—developing a system of cheap, easily accessible lots around the edge of the business district. These lots would be linked to the downtown by bus."

The idea has been tried out elsewhere. Boston, for example, has been creating parking lots on the outer reaches of its subway system. Whether this incipient movement is going to help to revive the nation's troubled public transit systems remains to be seen.

One thing is certain, however: There is fresh evidence to show that public transit is a much more important element than many people thought a few years back. Two recent studies have served to develop this point. One was a study of shopping habits in downtown and suburban Boston, made by Boston University; the second, . . . by Ohio State University, examines shopping habits in Seattle, Columbus, and Houston. In Boston it was found that only 22 per cent of people who go from suburbs downtown to shop do so by car. In Seattle 39 per cent, and in Houston and Columbus 55 per cent of the people said that they used a car the last time they went downtown to shop.

The trouble is that everyone's attention has been focused for so long on the problem of parking space that other problems have been neglected. Admittedly, merchants find parking the most galling and ever-present problem downtown. But parking is actually only a part of the problem, as is plainly shown in the Houston case.

More Than One Approach

Today, the experts in city planning have devised a whole series of approaches to the problem of urban renewal. These can be divided roughly into four main groupings:

Get people in and out quickly. The general idea here is to use all methods that can make the downtown area more accessible and to improve traffic conditions. You can improve public transit, build parking garages, improve traffic flow on existing streets, put expressways around town for traffic heading past the city, and put speedways into the city for traffic heading in and out.

Give the city back to people. Victor Gruen, the designer of the big Northland shopping center built by J. L. Hudson Company in suburban Detroit, urges the separation of pedestrians and vehicles where possible. One way is to create downtown shopping centers for foot traffic only, on the order of the new Lijnbaan shopping center in downtown Rotterdam. Cities could set aside whole blocks and streets as pedestrian malls during the daytime.

Use the land properly. This is, of course, a vast and complex problem, fraught with difficulties involved in land value, zoning, and other aspects of urban real estate. In essence, however, the idea is to use a city to the purpose for which it is best suited. It means, as a simple illustration, getting residential buildings out of industrial areas.

Rebuild the slums that constrict the center town. A theory is spreading among people involved in planning that a poor way to do this is to create what someone has called "ghettos for the financially underprivileged"—in other words, housing projects for low-income families. There have been attempts to create mixed projects. One such is the proposed Gratiot-Orleans project in Detroit, which would have everything in it from tall apartment buildings to garden apartments and even single-family houses. The project may also mix races.

This would seem to imply that urban renewal may mean the packing of more people downtown in congested areas. In reality, most projects are not planned to do this. Even if they were, it is unlikely that they could reverse the trend running toward decentralization in an atomic age. One major factor working for decentralization is the pressure being put on by the government to get military production out of the big centers that would be natural targets in an atomic war.

Economic developments are also still pushing strongly toward decentralization. Where industry goes, people go, too.

Merchants know this. They are not trying to check the vast movement of population out of downtown areas. Talbott puts his finger on the merchant's view when he asks, "Couldn't there be a peaceful and profitable coexistence between the central downtown and the suburban business area?"

Victor Gruen thinks that in reality there is no conflict between the downtowners and the decentralizers. "This conflict," he says, "is a phony." It diverts attention from the central fact, which is that the two—downtown and suburbs—are complementary parts of a whole. Both must be planned, or the whole retail machine will be distorted.

Gruen and other observers note that suburbia is susceptible to the same diseases and troubles that hobble the downtown area— and which spurred the move to the suburbs in the first place. Increasingly they are subject to congestion. White Plains, New York, one of the suburban centers outside New York City that developed early and rapidly, is now becoming uncomfortably congested. So are other suburban shopping centers, with the result that still farther-flung centers are developing around them.

Critical Mass

This sheds some light on the relationship between the city and the suburban center.

One of the problems is that the very things that make downtown what it is help to destroy it in the end—namely, people and traffic. Why do shoppers like to go downtown? The two studies, by Boston University and Ohio State, show clearly that shoppers like downtown areas because of the wide array of goods offered there, the range of sizes and colors, the range of prices. As might be expected, shoppers tend to go to their local shopping districts or centers for "convenience" items such as food and to

downtown areas for so-called "shopping" items—things such as
furniture, which people like to mull over before buying. In the
main, as the Boston survey showed, the more style is involved,
the more the downtown area is preferred.

The Ohio State study makes a further point that another step
is occurring: "Downtown facilities may increasingly serve specialized needs, and the servicing of more frequent and common needs
may be in the process of transfer to peripheral areas."

But could such functions be carried on if the downtown
rots away? Many major facilities—from big department stores
and theaters to museums and amusement centers—live only on
crowds. There is, as it were, a critical mass without which the
big center can't exist.

From the merchant's point of view, the question is not academic. His survival depends on the city's existence as a distribution center and as a center of activity. The department store, for
example, is becoming more and more a regional chain, in which
a number of small units cluster around a big central store that
handles warehousing, administration, and other services for them.

Says Talbott: "It is significant that the downtown store
remains as the main store, the parent institution without which
the branch could not long exist."

THE PARKING PROBLEM [6]

You drive in to the city to shop. For half an hour, you
cruise the streets looking for a place to park. Then, frustrated,
you look for room in a park-for-pay lot. You may have to scout
all over town before finding one that's not full. By the time you
step out of your car, you're tired and angry—and you vow never
to take your car to the city again. From now on, you'll shop in
the suburbs.

That decision, multiplied many thousandfold, means disaster
to America's large cities. They are losing their struggle against
the parking problem—and they aren't doing much about it.

[6] From "Solving That Parking Problem," by Charles T. McGavin, chief of
technical staff, District of Columbia Motor Vehicle Parking Agency, with Stacy
V. Jones, writer. *Collier's.* 130:34-7. November 1, 1952. Reprinted by
permission.

Yet they could. There's a way of winning it once and for all, within the next ten years and without municipal operation or investment. The method is to hit the problem with everything that will take cars off the streets: parking lots; ramp garages; mechanical garages; takedown skeleton structures; parking sections inside office buildings and department stores; and drive-in banks, restaurants, laundries, theaters and post offices.

Washington, D.C., has proved that this method works. In . . . six years the national capital has made a net gain of 18,000 off-street parking spaces and has caught up with the growth in traffic.

The District's Motor Vehicle Parking Agency, whose technical staff I head, has consistently been promoting the addition of more than 200 spaces each month. The pressure is letting up, and next year's tourist should find it easier to park. Within six or eight years we intend to add 25,000 more spaces, which ought to take care of the situation for some time. . . .

The parking industry is a huge business. Off-street parking facilities of all types, including those maintained by stores for their customers, represent a total investment across the nation of about $3 billion. Motorists pay annually about $200 million into parking meters. Although these figures sound large, business statistics and my own firsthand observations indicate there has been only a piddling improvement in the nation's parking capacity during the last decade. . . .

Meanwhile, the problem continues to grow. Car use has steadily increased. In 1923, when the automobile was "a pleasure car," usually jacked up and put on blocks for the winter, average annual travel was 7,500 miles; today it's 9,000. And I predict that by 1965, if the resourcefulness that went into development of the vehicle itself is applied to roadways and parking facilities, the average automobile will travel 18,000 miles a year.

There are now enough cars so that everybody in the country could sit down in them at once—one for every three and a half persons. In Los Angeles, which grew up after 1923, when the automotive revolution began, the ratio of cars to people is even higher. You could evacuate the entire population of that city on the front seats of its cars.

Further, the trend in car design is still toward longer, wider
and lower models. And don't blame the motor maker; it's a
matter of meeting public demand. . . . The parking problem
directly concerns the more than half of our population that now
live in America's 168 metropolitan areas. . . .

Both the central city and the "bedroom" areas are affected,
but in different ways. The city faces the loss of population and
revenue to the satellite areas if it can't provide space for automobiles. On the other hand, the city's parking problem often
presents an opportunity to the satellite community which has
cheap land available and can use free lots to attract business away
from the central area. Among communities that have made
notable use of parking to siphon customers out of big cities are
Silver Springs, Maryland, near Washington, and Kansas City,
Kansas, across the river from Kansas City, Missouri.

With the growth of population in the "bedroom" areas, the
use of automobiles for commuting has grown rapidly. In
Washington, for example, more than half the cars parked downtown are from outside the city. Naturally, too, the shopping
center has followed the migration to the suburbs. When the
housewife can park easily near home, she favors the branch store
in her own community.

The outward movement of business creates a serious tax
problem for the central area. In the average city, the downtown
section is roughly 1 per cent of the total area, yet it contributes
from 10 to 25 per cent of the real-estate tax revenues. If there
are sales and personal-property taxes, the yield is much greater.
Furthermore, a downtown section pays a lot more in taxes than it
gets back in services. Any drop in revenues has to be met by
homeowners and the citizenry in general.

What can the big cities do to solve their problem? It is
primarily a matter for municipal planning and encouragement,
rather than municipal investment and operation. You can't just
sit back and let private enterprise solve the problem in its own
way; you have to give both a helping hand and a prod. The city
can say to the [parking facility] operators, in effect, "We're ready
to give you every help we reasonably can; but, of course, if you
can't do it, we'll have to."

A first step, I should say, would be to establish a city parking agency, under one name or another. The temptation in any government is to set up a special committee and then forget about the problem. But an agency takes the responsibility for getting something done. Under state authorization, a number of cities are now organizing parking agencies. Baltimore has its Off-Street Parking Commission, established in 1948, which is doing an excellent job.

Once you have a staff, determine the city's stake in the parking problem's solution. Some taxpayers always object to spending money on parking studies until you show them that they'll have to pay more taxes unless something is done.

Next, chart the existing parking sites and their capacity in detail, and annually at least. In the District of Columbia we make an inventory of facilities about every nine months. We do it on foot, block by block, recording the size and shape of each lot or garage and giving it a rated capacity based on its method of operation.

You also need to know the demand. Your city probably has made basic surveys of the daily movements of people and cars, which can be supplemented by such methods as placing questionnaire cards in cars and interviewing drivers, and can be kept up to date by spot checks. . . .

Once you know how much additional space is needed and where, you can choose the best attack. The next step is a survey of potential parking sites—including, of course, any available municipal properties within walking distance of the stores and office buildings.

I have found that in major cities resistance to walking begins at about 500 feet and increases with the distance. People hate to go more than 750 feet from their cars for any purpose. In the District of Columbia we are aiming at a distance of 600 feet from parking facilities to key establishments. This is based on the preference of the shopper and not of the employee. Where parking is provided within 600 feet, we are confident that the Washington merchants can compete effectively with any of the suburban shopping centers. . . .

Almost every city has at least one site that's not of much use for anything but parking—perhaps a large plot down near the railroad tracks.

If the owner of a likely-looking property isn't personally interested in developing it for parking, the city agency can—with his permission—suggest such use to somebody else. And often the city can put a would-be operator in touch with a source of money—a bank, an insurance company or an individual. We occasionally arrange for operator to meet investor in our office. Some chain operators of parking garages provide everything—capital as well as engineering and management.

When somebody consults us about a specific site, we can suggest the most efficient installation, give him a design layout, estimate the land and construction costs and the probable yield, or even help break a bottleneck in negotiations.

Cooperation of the downtown merchants is, of course, necessary to a solution of a city's parking dilemma. Businessmen are usually suspicious at first of anything a city government tries to do. The argument most effective with a merchant is to point up how improved parking facilities will make his cash register jingle. Often he's so busy inside that he doesn't get a chance to see what's going on outdoors. I made a study of a Los Angeles store, which showed that purchases by people using its parking garage averaged $12.50 per trip. An average of one and three-quarters persons came per car, so each car brought $22 in sales. Since every parking stall was used by an average of 4.5 cars daily, each helped contribute $99 in sales. The 250-car garage therefore was an important factor in attracting $7 million worth of business annually.

Your city will probably have to modernize its building and zoning regulations to let parking expand. The District of Columbia building code was modified by reducing the required amount of automatic sprinkling so that six-story parking garages became economically feasible. Washington was the first city to recognize mechanical garages as a special type of building. Another code amendment made possible the use of skeleton steel structures. The National Board of Fire Underwriters, which had looked askance at parking garages as fire hazards, concluded that if off-street parking was not encouraged, the streets would be so crowded that fire apparatus would have difficulty in getting to fires. . . .

We must not neglect the old-fashioned parking lot, the chief reliance for the present of even the big cities. But mechanical garages, which require only narrow frontage and a minimum number of employees, hold the greatest promise for the future. I look for bold new designs. . . .

In addition to the garages of standard steel-and-concrete construction, with floors connected by ramps, skeleton steel frames are available in prefabricated form. These have the advantage of being demountable, so that they can be used on leased land and moved when there's a better use for the site.

Other cities might well promote a building design like Washington's unique Cafritz Building, where you "park at your desk." That is, a businessman drives up a ramp in the core of the building, parks his car on his own floor and walks a short distance to his office. The garage, with a half mile of highway, is in the center, and all the offices on the perimeter.

Underground parking is more spectacular than practical if you have to buy the land and excavate for the garage. If a public site is available in the right place to be leased at nominal rent, the cost may be justified. . . .

"Fringe parking" has been adopted with success in cities whose streetcar and bus lines have granted reduced fares. The term indicates the use of a series of lots outside the business area which can be reached by surface lines. The city-bound driver parks on the outskirts and takes a transit line the rest of the way. If, however, besides the time lost in transferring, the driver must pay a round-trip transit fare of thirty cents or more, plus even a nominal charge for parking, the fringe idea isn't attractive.

"Dual purpose" developments, combining stores and garages, have often rewarded their builders. Trustees of the Girard Estate in Philadelphia, for instance, demolished a block of run-down buildings in a fashionable shopping district and replaced them with modern shops on the first and second floors, devoting the upper stories and roof to parking. The whole neighborhood has now, as a result, been rejuvenated.

Los Angeles has made excellent use of the rear-door idea, particularly along Wilshire Boulevard, the Fifth Avenue of the West. The I. Magnin Company, for one, has one customer entrance on the boulevard and another entrance at the back, where parking space is available. But the back door, which is used by 80 per cent of the shoppers, is breath-taking in its beauty.

Among the smaller communities, Quincy, Massachusetts, was the pioneer in such development. It turned land between stores and railroad tracks into parking lots, and the stores put their display windows on that side. Garden City, Long Island, when it had less than 10,000 population, began to provide car space, and now has over half a dozen rear-door lots with a total capacity of 2,000 cars.

Towns that want to attract customers can often buy land, surface it properly for about $150 per car, so that the total cost per space is around $400. If the town wants to use meters, the investment can be recovered very shortly. Income from a parking meter has been estimated at $100 per year. . . .

Big cities now face their worst competition in the new "regional shopping centers." A promoter buys from 10 to 25 acres of baseball diamond, golf course or rural acreage strategically placed near housing developments and major highways and converts it into a complete "downtown" shopping area, leaving nothing to happenstance. For example, take the Hecht Company's Parkington Development in Arlington, Virginia, across the Potomac from Washington: customers can walk into the Hecht store from a five-level, 2,000-car parking building. Other stores cluster around.

The cities have been saved by the bell three times. Once was in 1933 when the depression stopped suburban building. The second time was in 1941, when war preparation cut material supplies. And the third time was in 1951, when rearmament again brought restrictions. If enough downtown parking isn't provided by 1961, our big cities will have to surrender, and reconcile themselves to a permanently slower tempo. And that's just another way of saying they'll strangle to death.

PUBLIC PARKS [7]

"What are parks for?" It sounds like a rhetorical question. Who indeed, in principle at least, does not want parks at a time of unprecedented population growth, youth and age problems, increasing urban congestion, rapid expansion of suburban sub-divisions, disappearance of natural shorefront, shrinkage of the great outdoors, frantic pushing of car sales, soaring air travel and water shortages? You might as well ask who doesn't want lungs and fresh air to fill them. . . .

Recreation today is big business. Public recreation occupies a larger and larger slice of the budget pie—of all budget pies, Federal, state, municipal. American municipalities, including counties, towns, cities and villages, with few exceptions have always had inadequate parks and playgrounds. Today when they are bursting their seams we wake up to discover the ap-palling bill which must be paid to make up for past smugness, stupidity, neglect and selfishness.

Statistics in this field are highly misleading. Acreage is not the measure. A municipality may have a large percentage of so-called green belts and big parks, but these may be in the wrong places or not where they are most needed. It may have parks but inadequate neighborhood playgrounds.

Today sound planning demands both play areas and small parks with facilities for all groups in or near housing subdivi-sions and slum clearance projects, and athletic fields at new schools shared by the education and park authorities. There must be not only municipal recreation near home, but state recreation on an even larger scale in the suburbs and the national government must increasingly save and maintain historical and natural marvels.

We must pay more attention to the several age groups and to passive as distinguished from active recreation. Older people must be allowed to relax and read without getting hit on the head by baseballs or jarred out of their wits by Comanche Indians and Hopalong Cassidys, not to speak of gangs of young

[7] From "The Moses Recipe for Better Parks," article by Robert Moses, Park Commissioner, New York City. New York *Times Magazine.* p 13+. January 8, 1956. Reprinted by permission.

thugs requiring firm police control. Museums which go with parks must be rebuilt, revivified, expanded and made accessible, attractive and fascinating to hitherto unguessed numbers.

Our zoos must be multiplied. Art in parks has been not so much neglected as exploited by dubious talent. We require game refuges in cities as well as in the open country. We need large forest reserves not only to protect our climate and watersheds, but for camping by families which must have at least rudimentary shelter and cannot live in tents, lean-tos and shacks open to the elements. We need more parkways leading to the open spaces, parkways which are in effect ribbon parks with occasional attractive stopping places on their borders, and expressways open to mixed traffic and built to something like parkway standards.

Now who can possibly be against such a program which is so logical, so indispensable, so popular, so undeniable in principle? I'll tell you.

Everybody with an axe of his own to grind. Every selfish vested interest. Politicians who endorse the program but don't like its application if some votes may be lost in the process. Arthritic toes which get stepped on. Ultra-conservatives who like almost everything near and dear to them as it is, but would go along with change elsewhere. Special groups and interests for this, but against that. Nature fanatics. Hunters and fishermen who want 2 million acres of the Adirondacks to themselves. Taxpayers' organizations which welcome progress if it doesn't cost anything. Real estate boards which concede that parks raise surrounding values generally but not at this particular location. Civic organizations which demand another exhaustive survey. Legislative and other committees with their hangers-on and camp followers who see the need of prolonged hearings and heavy reports. Planners who demand a bolder, more comprehensive approach. Pundits with their "on the one hand, on the other hand" opinions which leave the reader bewildered and confused. Pessimists who say too little and too late.

Why go on? It remains a fact that no major park acquisition is accomplished except over the dead bodies of obstructionists. . . .

I do not despair of providing parks to keep pace with the population, in spite of our mistakes and deficiencies. The cost will be burdensome, but there will be more people to pay the bills. We shall have to adopt new and radical devices in the interest of posterity. For example, we shall have to buy private golf clubs, game refuges, shooting preserves and big estates for future parks, and perhaps let the present owners live on them for ten or twenty years, perhaps tax free. Outside of Staten Island, there is only one real private golf club left in New York City. They keep moving farther out in the suburbs. A private shooting preserve within fifty or sixty miles of the city is an expensive anachronism waiting only for a big offer from an eager realtor.

There must be some millionaires in the suburbs who will cooperate if not dedicate on reasonable terms. There must be some who don't have subdivision plans tucked away in the safe deposit box showing how Junior can cash in when the old man dies. There must be near-by clubs where the members realize that the tax collector is upon them, places where the neighbor's children are flushing the pheasants and killing the tame ducks with bean shooters. And finally there is, praises be, that last most drastic weapon of the people where a great public purpose can be served in no other way, the power of eminent domain. . . .

Prosperity without prudent control, physical growth without regulation in the common interest, movement without plan or purpose, pursuit of happiness with no common objective, prolongation of life without cultivation of leisure, this is not civilization. Parks are the outward visible symbols of democracy. That in my book is what they are for.

DEFENSE CONSIDERATIONS IN CITY PLANNING [8]

Defense considerations have become primary considerations in American city planning. The United States is an urban nation, drawing its strength from the productive power of its cities. To the extent that they are vulnerable to enemy attack, the nation is vulnerable.

[8] From statement by the American Institute of Planners. *Bulletin of the Atomic Scientists.* 9:268. September 1953. Reprinted by permission.

The emergence of nuclear weapons vastly more destructive than any hitherto developed makes necessary a complete reassessment of the forms that cities must take to continue their vital role in our national life. The old rules are no longer valid.

The new weapons make possible the sudden and complete destruction of large urban centers. They place in the hands of potential enemies a means of striking swift and crippling blows against the cities in which our productive power is massed and so against the nation that depends on them.

Those cities should and can be a source of sustaining strength. They are at present a terrifying source of weakness. They can be planned and developed in forms that deny profitable targets to an attacker and so can discourage attack. As now constituted, they make profitable targets for modern weapons and thereby invite attack.

Whether any nation is at the moment ready to launch such attacks against us is not material. The means for launching them are known and the necessary resources are available to any modern industrial society that cares to develop them.

The danger may or may not be imminent but it is potential and probably will continue to overshadow all that we do for generations. The President has said, *we live in an age of peril.* Theree is no time to lose in preparing for that life if we are to live it as free men. . . .

During the 1940-1950 decade, the population of the United States increased by 19 million people, but 15 million of that increase went into its metropolitan areas. Six million were added to the central cities of those areas. Thus, in the decade that witnessed the birth of nuclear weapons, the nation became progressively more vulnerable to their effects.

At the end of that decade, there were 4,284 urban places in the continental United States, but only 232 of them had populations above 50,000 and so, on the basis of their size, were likely targets for even the smallest atomic weapons. If the nation's entire urban population had been distributed evenly among the 4,284 places, each would have had a population of only 22,520 and a total of 2,640 persons employed in manufacturing. . . .

Any such distribution of the nation's urban population is, of course, an impractical extreme and an unnecessary one. But the present massing of people in a few score major urban concentrations is also an extreme and one the nation cannot safely live with.

Somewhere between those two extremes is a form of urban organization that will provide an optimum combination of immunity to damage from airborne weapons and efficiency and economy in producing the goods, services, and amenities of modern urban living.

It is a prime responsibility of the science of city planning, working with other technologies concerned with urban development and national defense, to define that form of organization and to develop the procedures by which it may be attained within the framework of American institutions.

The American Institute of Planners endorses the efforts of the Federal Government . . . to define the nature of the problem and to outline measures for its solution.

It urges additional research to determine more fully:

The characteristics which make areas of urban development remunerative targets for nuclear weapons and those which make them unremunerative;

Ways in which the latter can be combined with characteristics that promote efficient industrial production, economical city operation and pleasant urban living;

Procedures by which new urban development can be given the combined characteristics so outlined; and

Procedures by which existing urban development that fails to possess these characteristics can be remodeled to more nearly approach them.

Reducing the nation's vulnerability to attack is as much a national defense measure as is the provision of military forces to repel attack. Both are a basic responsibility of the Federal Government. The Institute urges the Federal Government to provide strong and continuing leadership in this field and to recognize reduction of vulnerability as a prime consideration in all construction and development projects which it undertakes or for which it provides financial or other assistance.

To be successful, such leadership must be exercised in a way that stimulates state and local governments to prepare and carry out constructive land use plans for the development of all major metropolitan areas. Unless there is a clear, consistent, and authoritative national policy with respect to the location of industry, the necessary planning and action at the local level will be inhibited.

The American Institute of Planners does not claim competence in military measures of national defense, but it holds this fact self-evident, that the best way to prevent attacks upon this country is to deprive potential enemies of targets that will make such attacks profitable to them.

The grave danger that now confronts us stems from the fact that our productive strength is at present so distributed as to facilitate destruction. A relatively small expenditure of enemy effort, armed with modern weapons, could do frightful damage. The situation is an open invitation to attack, and plain common sense dictates that it should be remedied with all possible dispatch.

III. AN ANALYSIS OF PLANNING

EDITOR'S INTRODUCTION

Planning is a profession, but it is a relatively new one whose limits are not yet clearly defined. In essence, planners are advisers to the elected responsible community officials. But as planning techniques are more universally adopted, communities appear more and more willing to accept the planner's advice as an organized and firm procedure to which all must adhere.

The underlying theme of this section is that community planning is both possible and desirable for any community—small or large, new or old, expanding or contracting.

This section first deals with a broad definition of community planning, followed by a brief history of the subject in its American aspects. This in turn is followed by a dissection of the city plan itself by one of the nation's growing number of recognized eminent planners — Harland Bartholomew. Next, another distinguished planning "elder statesman," Henry S. Churchill, discusses some aspects of the philosophy of planning. Finally, another authority comments on the present status of planning in America.

WHAT IS PLANNING? [1]

City planning is the process of substituting foresight for hindsight. Through the planning process, a community attempts to anticipate future developments and plan for those anticipated developments. No city is too small to plan, nor is it necessary that a community be a growing one for planning to be desirable. Change is a phenomenon common to all communities and planning can serve a very useful purpose by guiding change into desirable patterns of community development. Planning also can

[1] From *Planning Your Community*, pamphlet by Lyle C. Kyle, executive secretary, Woodbury County Taxpayers Conference, Sioux City, Iowa. (Citizen's Pamphlet Series no 16) Governmental Research Center. University of Kansas. Lawrence, Kansas. 1955. p 9-14, 18-22. Reprinted by permission.

help to solve current problems. The mere process of thoroughly studying your community in relation to recognized standards of desirable community development may well provide solutions to some of those problems.

Planning enables a community to put its desire on paper, mobilize public opinion behind the desired program of city improvement, and take the legal steps necessary to accomplish the program.

Many people confuse "planning" and "zoning." The terms do not mean the same thing. Zoning is but a part of planning, a method of implementing that part of a city plan which is concerned with land uses. The zoning ordinance specifies where new homes can be built, where industries can be located, and where the retail businesses should be. It does not preclude the location of a business or residence in a community but guides the location into areas where similar uses exist.

It might be said that city planning is similar to personal planning, but on a community rather than an individual basis. To help illustrate the point, two examples of personal planning can be used to parallel city planning. A family building a new home gives considerable thought to, among other things, landscaping and financing. The purpose of landscaping is to secure the most efficient use of the lot while beautifying it. Considerable planning must go into the process of planting the right kind of tree in the correct location. The tree must be placed in a position where shade will be most beneficial. It must be placed where the roots will not interfere with sewer or water lines or where streets or sewer repairs will not result in the destruction of the tree. Consideration must be given to the effect the tree will have on the neighbors' property. Lastly, the tree should be placed where it will not hamper activities of the family in the yard. Thus many factors are considered when planning the location of a tree in the yard.

The same principle is present in using zoning as a tool for city planning. The use of the land in the city is important. It is not desirable to have a junk yard located in a predominantly residential area. Experience has shown that individuals do not always consider all factors related to land use; as a result communities have developed the process of zoning to ensure that important factors are considered before locating businesses, residences, and other land uses. Consequently, a zoning ordinance retricts a predominantly residential area for residential purposes only. Other areas in the city are better suited for commercial or industrial uses and are so designated by a zoning ordinance.

To return to the comparison of individual and community planning, finance is of prime importance to a family building a home. For this reason, many families build a home that can be expanded or altered at a future time to fit the family's desires. The new home may include an unfinished upstairs, a basement with possibilities for a recreation room, and plans for an attached garage.

The family analyzes its resources and then budgets for these future improvements. The cost of each improvement, the relative need for each improvement, and the desire for each one are considered in arriving at a plan for the completion of all the improvements over the next few years.

Planning a capital improvement program for the city involves a similar process. Once the city's resources have been determined, the needs and desires of the community analyzed, then the city adopts a planned capital improvement program.

Many times the question is asked, "What is a city plan?" There is no hard and fast rule which specifies that a written document containing nine specific topics is a city plan, while a document with only seven topics is not. Rather, the city plan is an expression of the needs and desires of a community. Normally, however, the following subjects are thought of as proper parts of a city plan in small communities: (1) street system; (2) parking and traffic; (3) public buildings; (4) public health; (5) schools; (6) zoning; (7) recreation; (8) subdivision regulations; (9) land use and population characteristics; and (10) finance.

Why Should We Plan?

Perhaps the best way to answer that question is to cite examples of what happens when we do not plan.

How often have we driven down a street in one of our . . . communities and wondered why the city didn't provide for wider streets? Or, perhaps we have asked ourselves why business enterprises locating in the downtown district weren't required to provide off-street parking space. As a result of the development of city planning, many communities now require any new business or residence being constructed to provide off-street parking space in proportion to the number of customers or the number of people residing in a residence.

How often have we heard citizens of a community ask what can be done when a slaughter house locates its new plant in a residential neighborhood? As a result of the development of zoning as a tool of city planning, zoning ordinances can now restrict the uses that can be made of land within various areas of the city. This is done by setting out certain parts of the city to be used for industrial uses, commercial uses, and residential uses. Zoning does not prohibit the location of an industrial or other intensive use within a city, but rather restricts the area in which that use can be located.

In this era of rapidly increasing urban populations, citizens of a community often ask why the school board did not anticipate the increased load on the public school system when it asked for money to build a new school, and upon building that new school found that it was overcrowded on the day of opening. Planning may not solve that problem completely, but in analyzing past and present population trends in the city, the potential school enrollment in future years would be studied carefully in order to anticipate future school plant needs as accurately as possible. To illustrate further the desirability of city planning, we can cite the fact that many times new subdivisions are designed and built without regard to the existing street pattern, desirable building setbacks and side yard spaces, the size and type of sewer and water lines and other utilities necessary for day-to-day living in an urban community. Through subdivision regulations, each new subdivider can be required to secure approval of his plat from the planning commission before proceeding. [A plat is a plan of a town site, division of land, or the like—Ed.] In this way the planning commission can insure that new subdivisions fit into the general pattern of the community.

Probably many communities feel that they are too small to warrant planning. On the contrary, no city is too small to plan. In the first place, modern-day communities can never be sure when something may occur that will cause them to double, triple, or even quadruple their population within a period of a few months. When this happens, having a planning commission and a plan will help that community grow in a logical and orderly fashion. . . .

One factor that should not be overlooked by any city planning commission is that the community for which it is going to plan is already there; it is a physical reality. Seldom do we get the chance to lay out a new city and then begin to build. Rather, we must work with existing communities, accept what is there, and try to improve what will be there in the future. It would be desirable if we could remake many of our cities, but few, if any, urban communities can economically afford to remake themselves. Consequently, we are working with what can be done to improve a community in the future.

City planning will not work miracles overnight and perhaps not over a longer period of time. But in the course of a generation, planned growth in a community should help to make a better community in which to live, work, and play. . . .

Once the city governing body has decided to proceed with planning the development of the city, what is the process for accomplishing this end?

Appointing the Planning Commission

Naturally the first step is to pass an ordinance creating a planning commission; then comes the appointment of the membership. [Composition of planning boards varies from state to state, but in Kansas, for example] . . . a city planning commission must be composed of at least seven but not more than fifteen members. The only requirements as to membership are that the members be taxpayers and reside in the community except that two members must live outside the corporate limits of the city but within three miles of the city limits.

The mayor of the city appoints the members with the consent of the governing body. Terms of the members are three years, with the first appointments to be made in such a manner that terms of membership shall be staggered.

Aside from the statutory limits upon the size of the planning commission, it is desirable that the membership be large, preferably the full fifteen members, thus providing for a fairly wide representation. All geographical areas of the city should be represented.

Many planning commissions are heavily weighted with business executives, realtors, architects, engineers and lawyers. Certainly those groups should be represented but not to the exclusion of others. Minority groups, the ministry, school teachers or administrators, labor, the medical profession, women, the senior citizen group, young people, and civic organizations should be represented on the commission. It would be desirable to have a representative of the press as a member, but newspaper men may feel that they cannot present an unbiased picture of the proceedings of the planning commission if they are a member of that group. At the least, a member of the press should be invited to attend the meetings of the commission since the press certainly wields considerable influence in a community.

Members should not be selected for professional competence alone. An understanding of the city and its problems, of the contributions that planning can make to an improved community, broad vision, demonstrated genuine and unselfish interest in the public welfare, integrity and soundness of judgment, and prestige in the community are important considerations.

The first step that a planning commission should take in preparing to draw up a city plan is to inventory the community and analyze the results of that inventory. There are several methods for making such an inventory. For example, a private consulting firm can be employed to prepare a city plan for the community. This method short-circuits the other steps to be detailed in this outline, but it does result in providing the city with a ready-made answer to its planning problems. The private consulting firm will conduct the actual study of the city, analyze the results of the study, and draw up a plan and present it to the planning commission and the governing body. This plan will undertake to show what the community is, what it should be in the future, and the methods by which it can reach that goal. A second method is to employ such public agencies as may be available to make an inventory of your community, analyze that inventory, and suggest alternative solutions to problems. However, such agencies will not provide a detailed city plan for the community. That step is to be performed by the city planning commission itself. A third method is to do the whole job without outside help. Certainly this latter method would be the most desirable from the standpoint of the community and its members Until communities are willing to perform this function themselves, city planning will not realize its full potential.

The area of study to be embraced by any of these groups should be determined by the city planning commission and should represent the general interests and ideas of the citizenry in regard to its community problems. For purposes of illustration we shall list a few of the problems that seem to be common to many communities and probably would be studied in the planning process. These would include problems relative to the street system of the city, the school system, utilities, public buildings, parking, zoning, transit system if any, the economy of the community, public health, recreation, and others that might be especially important to a given city.

Active citizen participation should be encouraged in order that the inventory of community problems represents not only the planning commission's ideas as to problems but also those of the entire community. There is no proven method of accomplishing this step with guaranteed success. Civic groups, parent-teacher associations, church groups, and other organized groups in a community should be sounded out for their ideas. Perhaps this can be arranged by having a member of the planning commission attend meetings of these groups to discuss with them the idea of city planning and the problems that the planning commission has, and in turn searching for ideas that the group may have. Public hearings by the planning commission are not very successful since people seldom appear to discuss public issues. If the members of the planning commission represent all economic and social interests in the community as well as the geographic division of the city, perhaps each member, by discussing city problems with the people in his area, can obtain some of the community's ideas. Unquestionably the degree of success with which citizen participation and support is secured will determine the success or failure of a city plan once that plan is adopted by the governing body. Without active citizen support throughout the planning process, a plan may well be formulated that does not represent community desires and interests and thus will not have the support needed to carry it out.

Once the community inventory has been completed, and the results analyzed, the next step in the planning process is to draw up a detailed city plan outlining the needs and desires of the community relative to each segment of the city plan. In large part, the drawing up of the city plan represents the process of arriving finally at a decision as to what should be done about schools, streets, parking, subdivision regulation, and zoning, and putting those decisions on paper along with the background material to explain the conclusions which have been reached and which are presented as a plan. [See "Elements of a City Plan" in this section, below.]

The next step as far as the city planning commission is concerned is to present its recommended plan to the city governing body. The city planning commission is an advisory agency so far as drawing up and carrying out the plan is concerned. Once a plan has been adopted and implementation is under way, the city planning commission should study and make recommendations on proposed changes in the adopted plan.

While it is true that the city governing body, rather than the planning commission, is the final authority, this does not mean that once a city plan is drawn, the function of the planning commission is ended. Certainly that is not the case. It is doubtful that any city will ever devise a plan which will stand the test of time unchanged. Planning is a continuing process and the planning commission should be continually involved in studying and recommending changes and adjustments in the adopted plan.

Another word of caution about the function of a planning commission and its relationship to the city governing body: It is not unusual to hear the thought expressed that a city planning commission is doing its job properly—that it meets and functions whenever the city commission has a problem for it to consider. This thought expresses a very limited view of the proper responsibilities and scope of action of a planning commission. City planning commissions are not, or at least should not be, created solely for the purpose of considering pressing problems presented to them at irregular intervals by city governing bodies. Unfortunately, it seems to be true that some city governments have created planning commissions for the primary purpose of relieving, temporarily at least, the pressures upon themselves to solve difficult or controversial public problems. Planning commissions established and functioning upon this basis cannot provide the continuous attention and positive leadership which is needed in order to work toward the most acceptable plan for the orderly growth and improvement of the community. The planning commission should have regular meetings at periodic intervals, and should study any city problem which the members feel should be studied. The commission should be a continuing focal point for the efforts of all citizens in building the best city possible.

A GLANCE AT HISTORY [2]

Washington and Jefferson were almost our first city planners. They spent much time and thought in considering the character and design of the capital city to be built upon the site on the Potomac River selected by Congress. While Jefferson was Ambassador to France, he obtained plans of various prominent cities in Europe and sent these to Washington together with his comments and suggestions. The final design for the capital city was

[2] From *Development and Planning of American Cities*, booklet by Harland Bartholomew, city planner, St. Louis, Missouri. (Carnegie Press Occasional Papers no 1) Carnegie Institute of Technology. Pittsburgh, Pennsylvania. 1950. p 4-13. Reprinted by permission.

prepared by a French engineer whom they employed for this purpose. It is of some significance that this man, Pierre Charles L'Enfant, was an engineer. He combined the various proposals into a pleasing and harmonious if not a fully complete functional design.

L'Enfant's plan of Washington was a bold vision for a great capital city laid down in a virtual wilderness. Its central feature was a wide mall extending for a mile and a half eastward from the Potomac River to a commanding hill site on which was placed the Congress House. A short cross axis provided for the location of the President's Home to the north on another high point commanding a fine view of the Potomac River valley. At the intersection of the two axes was to be a great monument— now the noble and beautiful Washington Monument. . . .

For almost a century the plan of Washington was considered to be too grandiose, too broad in scale. Half a century or more after its founding we learn of residents and visitors speaking of the community as "the city of magnificent distances."

L'Enfant made the fantastic prediction that the city would attain a population of 200,000 persons in one hundred years, and the scale of his plan was determined by this estimate. Washington was started in the year 1800, and it is extremely interesting to note that the population of the city as revealed by the Federal census of 1900 was 231,000 persons. Now, after but one half century of additional growth, the population of Washington and its environs is approximately 1.4 million persons.

Since Washington was planned as a capital city, more or less in the grand manner, it is not surprising that other American cities did not generally follow its example. Major Ellicott, engineer associated with L'Enfant, subsequently made plans for several small cities in Pennsylvania and western New York. While the early plans of several of these smaller towns and even a few larger cities such as Buffalo and Detroit reflect the type of design used in the Washington plan, the great majority of American cities were inspired more by William Penn's plan for the city of Philadelphia. Judged by total influence, William Penn was indeed our greatest city planner.

The Philadelphia plan consisted of a gridiron of streets running east and west from river to river (these streets being named for various trees), and north and south (numbered streets) paralleling the rivers. Interspersed at regular intervals throughout the gridiron were shown small parks. The central motif in this design consisted of a great plaza in the center of which was to be located the city hall, and with a very wide street extending both north and south and east and west therefrom (Broad Street and Market Street as we now know them). The site was a relatively small level area, and the plan, at least for the time and under the particular conditions then existing, was functionally good. It was designed more to meet the needs of a commercial city, with commerce along the waterfront and with areas for quiet, pleasant living in the center part of the community.

Penn's plan for Philadelphia had a widespread appeal because of its simplicity. It had a profound influence in the initial planning of a very large number of our American cities. As in Philadelphia, the sites of most of our early cities were level areas on rivers. Their small original plans were reasonably well conceived and functional in design, at least for the times and conditions then existing. Frequently there was a wide levee and often a park at the riverfront. There was a town square and a site for a court house, church, and other public buildings. The scale of the plan was in keeping with immediate foreseeable needs.

For at least three quarters of a century the United States remained predominantly an agricultural nation. Our cities experienced limited growth, and hence there were few serious planning problems. It is difficult to realize that as late as 1870 there were but three cities which had attained a population of 300,000 persons—New York, Philadelphia and St. Louis. Thereafter, with the coming of the so-called industrial age, the number of cities increased rapidly, and the influx of population to urban areas exceeded anything previously known in world history. By 1900 there were nine cities of over 300,000 population, and by 1940 there were thirty cities of this size. . . .

So rapid was the process of urbanization that by the turn of the century there was increasing public interest and concern about the planning of our cities. The early city plans were outgrown and no new designs made in anticipation of either current or future growth. "Additions" and "subdivisions" had been and were being added to the original city plan in such numbers that they far exceeded the area covered by the original plan. This produced an enormous patchwork and a hodgepodge of development from which virtually all American cities have been unable to extricate themselves. Unfortunately, there was little or no experience to use as a guide, and we became so engrossed in growth for growth's sake that we failed to define objectives and thus attempt to control the form and character of urban growth. Our cities also were unattractive as compared with European standards, and this caused much concern among the more esthetically inclined citizens. It was discovered further that the incidence of crime and disease was greater in the highly congested urban areas where our first slums were beginning to appear.

By 1910 the several groups concerned with these growing problems of cities united to form the National Conference on City Planning. From this time forward we began to develop what now has become a fairly well established science and art of city planning. Our scientific knowledge of the characteristics of urban growth is now quite broad. We have gone far in developing planning techniques. Our knowledge and our skills have far outrun our ability to apply and use them effectively, however.

An exceedingly well prepared comprehensive city plan for San Francisco, prepared by Daniel Burnham, was published immediately preceding the great earthquake and fire in 1905. This seemed like an act of Providence. Unfortunately, the plan was ruthlessly ignored in the scramble to rebuild. A comprehensive city plan for St. Louis was published in 1907. It was ignored by city officials. A monumental city plan for Chicago was published in 1909. . . . These were all the products of voluntary citizen groups interested and concerned in the future welfare of their communities. The motives and intentions were of the highest order, but something was wrong in the body politic.

The lack of immediate acceptance and implementation of these plans to direct the processes of urban development revealed a broad chasm between city planning design on the one hand and effective official action on the other. It was discovered that citizen committees, no matter how prominent, could not bring about the planning or replanning of American cities by voluntary action. Something more was needed. The mayor and the city council did not share the enthusiasm of the citizens committees. Without official sanction no city plan could be carried out.

Next steps turned to the creation of official city planning commissions within the corporate structure of government in the hope that this would bring about a happy combination of good planning and official acceptance and execution of those plans. Thus in 1912 city planning commissions were appointed by municipal authorities in St. Louis, Missouri, and in Newark, New Jersey. Today there are some 1200 to 1500 city planning commissions in various cities and towns.

The creation of official city planning commissions stimulated considerable planning activity. Comprehensive city plans were prepared and some were published in quite a number of cities. Some of these were broad in concept, functionally sound, and well adapted to existing conditions. While cities possessed many of the necessary powers to acquire land and to carry out public improvements, there was again found to be a pronounced gap between city planning design on the one hand and official acceptance and execution on the other. The mere presence of a city planning commission within the structure of government did not persuade most city officials of the desirability and necessity of following the city plans. There were some exceptions, of course, and in a few communities the process of controlling new growth was accepted and inaugurated, even though there was but limited action in carrying out the larger and more expensive projects for over-all community redesign and reconstruction. Our vision and our ambitions exceeded our powers of achievement. . . .

The introduction of the automobile at this formative stage of city planning action had a most disruptive effect. Potentially, at least, the scale of the American city was suddenly and radically changed. Even today, some two decades later, we can scarcely appraise the full impact of the automobile upon the form and character of the American city. It has made possible a physical expansion of the average city of not less than 1000 per cent. Its decentralizing force accelerates the development of central area slums and blighted districts. It fosters speculative development over vast areas in which there is as yet little or no effective control of standards of development or over-all comprehensive city plans. . . . The automobile has disrupted and virtually exploded the city fully as much as would an atomic bomb could its force be spent gradually.

Prior to 1930 our American cities had grown so rapidly that their future growth seemed unlimited. The great financial depression of the 1930's brought about an abrupt and shocking end to this concept. Twice during the 1930-1940 decade there were shifts of population away from the larger cities, chiefly because of unemployment. It was discovered that a progressively declining birth rate was bringing about a prospective stabilization of national population, which, in turn, would sharply limit the future growth of cities. The intervention of World War II and a suddenly increased birth rate have again stimulated population growth in cities, but it is generally agreed that future prospective increase in urban populations is now definitely restricted within foreseeable limits.

ELEMENTS OF A CITY PLAN [3]

For some thirty-five or forty years we have talked about city plans for American cities. This seems an appropriate time to consider our present understanding of the term "city plan," how it is made, and how it is or should be used.

There are several points of view. The civil engineer approaches the matter from the standpoint of the water supply, sewers, storm drainage, utilities, streets, transportation and terminals. The sociologist is concerned with housing, population

[3] Reprint of article entitled "The Plan—Its Preparation, Composition and Form," by Harland Bartholomew, city planner, St. Louis, Missouri. *American Planning and Civic Annual, 1951.* American Planning and Civic Association. Washington, D.C. 1951. p 97-102. Reprinted by permission.

density, parks and recreational facilities. The architect is particularly interested in buildings (public and private) and the open spaces which not merely provide good setting but which supply much needed light and air. The economist is concerned with trends in employment and volume and type of business and industrial activity without which the city could not exist. These interests are not mutually exclusive, nor need they conflict. Coordination of these points of view is essential, however. A city plan is an instrument whereby the utilitarian, the social, the economic, and the esthetic are so synthesized and coordinated as to produce the most satisfactory result. A city is, or should be, a unit. Its composition and its living and working conditions will be best where there is a unified design—a carefully prepared city plan that guides new growth and redevelopment. New technology and concepts may require modification in the over-all unified design from time to time.

American cities have grown rapidly in recent decades and there have been marked changes in technological improvements. There has also been a marked change in concepts of social welfare and in both national and local economy. The science and the art of making a city plan is more difficult than in early years of less rapid growth and change. However, this does not justify procrastination. It emphasizes the need for greater effort and higher skill in the production of city plans.

Are we producing the good city plans that are required? Is the total development and growth of American cities being directed in accordance with well-designed city plans? At the risk of being charged with pessimism, it is doubtful if these two questions can be answered affirmatively. There are a few notable exceptions. One explanation of this failure is that we have become so interested in the several fields of endeavor that we have lost sight of our objective. We have become so interested in planning that we have failed to produce good city plans. Planning is not an end in itself. It is merely a means to an end. Planning for planning's sake is only a pleasant pastime. Have we not fallen into the error of making "studies," conducting "surveys," and collecting "data" without an honest and realistic follow-through to the end of making complete and comprehen-

sive city plans? Have we not been content with too many "outline" plans, plans that are tenuous and vague in nature? We
are building the city of tomorrow now—today. Any city plan
that is not definite, official and detailed will not permit us to
coordinate our individual buildings, sewer lines, parks, or schools
as each of these is built. And have we not fallen into another
error of preparing a zoning ordinance or a major street scheme
and deluding ourselves and the public into the belief that this
is a city plan? We all know that these are merely a part, a
relatively small part, of a comprehensive city plan.

The making of a reasonably complete and comprehensive
city plan is not as formidable a task as it may seem. The requirements are three in number, i.e., funds, technical services,
and the determination to see that the job is done. None of these
present unusual obstacles. City plan commissions are receiving
generous appropriations in most cities today because this work
has come to be recognized widely as a highly important function
of municipal administration. There is some shortage of technical
personnel, but it is not acute. The greatest deterrent appears to
be hesitation upon the part of public officials, planning commission members, and staff to knuckle down to the task of initiating
and completing all of the work required.

If the city plan is to be more than a collection of theoretical
ideas, it should be reduced to tangible form. The Standard City
Planning Enabling Act, which is our best present legal guide,
mentions the location, character and extent of streets, waterfronts,
parks, utilities, transportation, among other things, as appropriate subjects for consideration in the making of a city plan. This
act, and the several state acts which have used it as a model,
make no close specification or limitation of subjects. The Standard City Planning Act also refers to the maps, plates, charts and
descriptive matter which accompany the city plan in order to
make clear the purpose and intent of the specific physical improvements proposed. Here is where the social and economic
significance of the physical improvements may be explained.

Each city has individual characteristics peculiarly its own.
Public improvements such as streets, sewers, public buildings
and the like are needs common to all cities. The city plan for

each city necessarily must include recommendations for all these types of facilities. Before plans for these public improvements are made, it is important to prepare and analyze information regarding social and economic conditions and trends, to study the historic development of the city's site, and to examine facts about land use and population trends, among other things, in order to understand why the city has developed into its present particular form.

When the various studies and plans have been completed, it is necessary to consider ways and means of carrying out the city plan. This means integrating the administration of the city plan into the day-to-day processes of governmental action. It means analysis of present laws and ordinances with recommendations for such changes or additions as may provide for more effective administration. It also means an analysis of the city's financial practices in undertaking public improvements and the preparation of a capital expenditure budget with systematic annual review, so that the most needed public improvements will not be neglected in favor of those demanded by pressure groups.

A modern city plan, therefore, is divided into three sections, i.e., matters having to do with research and analysis, recommendations for physical improvements, and ways and means of carrying out the plan. Specific modern city planning programs, therefore, may consist of approximately sixteen specific subjects, as follows:

Matters Having to Do with Research and Analysis
1. Historical Background
2. Site Characteristics and Development
3. Social and Economic Characteristics
4. Population Growth, Density and Distribution
5. Land Use

Plans for Physical Improvements
6. Major Street Plan (Including Off-Street Parking and Land Subdivision Control)
7. Local Transit Facilities
8. Transportation—Rail, water and air
9. Water Supply, Sewers and Drainage

10. Park and Recreational Facilities and Public Schools
11. Zoning
12. Housing
13. Public Buildings and Publicly Owned Lands
14. The City's Appearance

Ways and Means of Carrying Out the Plan
15. Administrative Policy and Practice
16. Capital Expenditure Program

In some cities there may be special problems of such significance as to warrant special study and a special report as a vital part of the city plan. In other cities, there may be justification for some variations or departure from this list of subjects. The initial step therefore, is to prepare a program of subjects which, taken together, will comprise the comprehensive city plan. At this juncture, decision should also be made of the time required to complete the entire work. Normally, this will require approximately two years or slightly more in smaller cities, three to four years in larger cities, depending in part upon the amount of work heretofore completed and available.

Each of the several topics contained in the city plan program should be the subject of a special report containing all necessary recommendations, maps, charts and diagrams as an integrated part of the plan. Over a period of three years, for example, this means the production of reports at approximately two months' intervals. These reports should be considered as preliminary in form until such time as very nearly all of them have been completed, at which time all can be consolidated and coordinated into a single unified plan.

The responsibility for preparation of the comprehensive plan rests squarely upon the shoulders of the city plan commission. Until they have performed this function the commission should give little time or attention to other matters. It is the one reason for the existence of a commission, for without a plan, the ideas of a planning commission are no better than any other group of individuals. A city plan commission should devote itself almost exclusively to the production of a comprehensive plan and thereafter to its administration. The city plan of course should be a dynamic instrument and the commission should carry on studies with a view to periodic reviews and revision of the plan, or major sections thereof, when these are warranted by important changes in conditions and trends.

In most cities the members of planning commissions are citizens giving voluntary part-time service, plus certain city officials with important administrative duties. Since most of the members have limited time and can seldom profess to have technical city planning training, it is the duty of the staff under competent technical direction to prepare the first drafts of the reports comprising the comprehensive city plan. As these first drafts are completed, they should be reviewed by members of the city plan commission prior to publication as preliminary reports. Thus the reports will represent important local viewpoints held by leading citizens with special knowledge of the community, and also the highly significant judgment of the city engineer and those other officials that have special knowledge of local conditions.

Once the reports have been prepared in preliminary form they should be furnished to organizations and groups in various parts of the city and made the subject of discussion by neighborhood groups and community organizations. They should be publicized in other ways such as by newspaper stories, public addresses, or the use of other media.

Much has been said about citizen participation in the making of city plans. We can agree that the wider the public understanding, the greater will be the chances for public acceptance of the city plan. The preparation of a city plan is not strictly an amateur undertaking, however; the larger the city, the greater the necessity for technical service for analysis and design. Neither can it be said that a good comprehensive city plan can be produced by a large group of individuals in general meetings. True, agreement can be reached by such groups on important matters of policy or practice, and this is exactly how citizen participation in the preparation of a city plan should take place.

In each city there should be a citizens' plan association open to membership to any and all citizens interested in the plan of their city. My personal viewpoint is that a citizens' plan association should have special committees on each and every subject in the city plan program. I would go so far as to have the citizens' plan association make a study of and a report of the initial drafts of reports prior to their publication in preliminary form by the city plan commission. This would not necessarily constitute a delegation of authority by the city plan commission in the fulfillment of its responsibilities in plan preparation. Final decisions would rest with the plan commission itself. This procedure, however, would have the advantage of bringing the widest possible citizen viewpoint and participation into the preparation of the city plan in its earliest stages. There would of course be ample opportunity later for further consideration and discussion both by committees of the citizens' plan association and by groups and agencies of the community, out of which will come good recommendations and proposals for betterment in the plans contained in the preliminary reports.

Finally, after full discussion and consideration and after public hearings (which are usually required in most states), the various preliminary reports should be coordinated and synthesized and the plan should be formally adopted by the plan commission as the official comprehensive city plan. Without such action a plan is not much more than another municipal brochure about the city. It is not a sufficiently solid foundation upon which reliance can be placed by public agencies or by individuals, nor would it receive the required recognition by the courts.

The official plan should be published in attractive and substantial form and widely distributed. It should be a handbook to be easily and quickly referred to by all the many individuals, organizations, and agencies, both public and private, that are making improvements, designing buildings, investing money, or reaching decisions that affect the development of the city.

A city is not just a few big projects such as major airports, super-highways, or skyscrapers. Rather, it is an assembly of a great many relatively small things—individual homes, neighborhood parks, stores, churches and the like. Improved living and working conditions can come only through the coordination of all these things, both large and small—a coordination that must come when they are located and designed and before they are built. With a comprehensive city plan that is official, definite, detailed, and available for easy reference, the required coordination can be obtained, and all can participate in the exciting task of building a better city.

UNIVERSAL NEED FOR PLANNING [4]

"Our town doesn't need planning. It's growing nicely. Why, a hundred new jobs opened up here just last month."

Dennis O'Harrow, executive director of the American Society of Planning Officials, recently figured out what the advent of a hundred new families would mean to a medium-large city.

To begin with, it means about 450 new people. They will include about 100 children, 67 in grammar school, 33 in high school. This calls for 2.2 new rooms in grade school and 1.65 new rooms in high school, which will cost about $120,000. Four new teachers will have to be hired. The 100 families will add about $30,000 a year to the school budget.

Besides teachers, the city will need four fifths of a new employee in the police department and two thirds of a new fireman, upping the police budget by $4,510 and the fire department budget by $2,820.

All sorts of extra jobs will have to be done, too, from collecting taxes to collecting garbage. Add four new city employees at a total price of $12,000 to $15,000.

The water department must pump 10,000 gallons more each day. Traffic will be increased by 140 cars and trucks. And the city may have to add 500 new volumes to the city library, part of a visiting nurse and a fraction of a cell in the town jail.

More people, it seems, mean more problems, which mean more planning.

"We have no need for planning in our town. This town hasn't grown in twenty years. It's just plain standing still."

Growth isn't the only reason for planning. Planning can be a stimulant for towns that have stopped growing, too. By

[4] Reprint of article entitled "So Your Town Doesn't Need Planning." *Changing Times*, the Kiplinger magazine. 9:23. September 1955. Reprinted by permission.

making this town more attractive to new businesses and new
industries, planning might give it a new lease on life.

But even a town that looks changeless actually changes all
the time.

Frederick B. Clark of the Regional Plan Association of New
York cites an example. Poughkeepsie, New York, had a population of 40,000 in 1930. In 1940 the population still stood at
40,000. In 1950 it was just the same, 40,000 again.

Yet there was a difference. The 1950 Poughkeepsie had
2,200 more households than the 1930—smaller households, but
more of them. Thus it needed 2,200 more houses, shopping
facilities for 2,200 more households, parking spaces for 2,200
more cars. In fact, it needed 2,200 more of everything that is
measured in household units.

Needs of those dimensions can best be met by planning.

As Hugh R. Pomeroy, author of the nation's first county
zoning ordinance, has observed, "A city may not be growing,
but it certainly is not static. The only aggregation of population
that I know of that is static is that to be found in a cemetery."

PLANNING IN A FREE SOCIETY [5]

City planning is curious art, or profession, or business or
whatever it is. I think probably "profession" is the right word,
because it professes to do so much and accomplishes so comparatively little. This is not wholly the fault of the professors.
They do their best, but the odds are against them.

The odds are vested interest, public inertia, legal obfusca-
tion, financial inadequacy, governmental red-tape, and, neither
last nor least, lack of an objective for which to plan. Perhaps
city planning is too new a device to have developed an objective
or a philosophy; on the other hand perhaps we planners, mis-
educated as we are, do not know that in order to plan we must
look beyond tables of statistics.

It may seem odd to some of you that I even refer to city
planning as "new." Surely planning goes back to the oldest

    [5] From article by Henry S. Churchill, Consultant for Planning and Architecture,
Philadelphia, Pennsylvania. *Journal of the American Institute of Planners.* 20:
189-91. Fall 1954. Reprinted by permission.

cities of civilization. And too in historic times how about Peking, the Rome of Sixtus and the Paris of Haussmann, the New Towns of Palma Nuova and of Charleville, of Lima and Cartagena?

That was a different kind of planning. That was single-purpose physical planning, dictated planning. There was little economics in it, no sociology and certainly no democracy. It had little resemblance to our efforts at replanning and redevelopment. It was architecture, engineering and great art, and I sometimes think we need today a lot more architecture and engineering and more respect for them as art. We have to live with what is built, not with social case histories. . . . These have their place, but the place is in formulating the program, not in creating the design. A program is one thing, a design to be executed is another, and when that stage is reached the planner must be an architect and should be an artist. All the rest of city planning should lead up to that—the three dimensional thing we have to live in and with.

This is not the city beautiful, either, and that is where we again depart from the old city planning. The Paris behind the grand squares and the boulevards was—and is—largely a mess of foul old slums which, since we do not have to live with them, we call "picturesque." The once lovely and patrician cities of Charleville and Lima and all the once charming medieval towns have swollen and suppurated into horrible industrial blots. The culture that created them passed away and a new culture took over. That culture too is on its way out, and here we are today in a transition period and without any culture of our own trying to bring order out of the chaos.

That chaos is not only in our physical cities, it is in our economics, our social order, our schooling, our governments and politics, our attitude towards the values of living. What else are fascism and communism and nazism except the revolt of a cultureless people against unbearable chaos? Democracy is a process and slow: it is to the everlasting credit of our city-planners that they strive to work within the framework of democracy. . . .

Planning today is not much like the old city planning, which perhaps it might be well to call not "city planning" but "civic design." Today we are chiefly concerned with repairing the old cities, trying to make them suitable for living in an age of technological devices which were originally meant to make living easier but which seem to have had quite the contrary result. Even if we were given dictatorial powers I doubt if we could resolve the problem as quickly as we sometimes think we could. Suppose tomorrow you start in to do what you liked with Phila-delphia—what would you do? I'm sure I don't know what I would do. A city is a very complex organism, and must meet the needs and desires of all sorts of people, all sorts of business, all sorts of social requirements. The evils that we seek to eradicate are deeply a part of the complex, and physical change will not change the sources of evils, which are economic, social, human.

I do not think that the task of the planner is to accomplish social or economic reform: that way dogmatism lies, and authori-tarianism of whatever complexion, right, left or religious. The planner should try to understand the effect technology has on living, and to adapt the physical form of the city accordingly. The automobile, the airplane, the radio and television and atomic fission have changed the mode of living profoundly, yet we are biologically the same creatures and require much the same as we always have in the way of quiet, relaxation, family associa-tion, friends. The planner's job is to fit the old essential needs into a framework that will take care of the new mechanism, so that we can go from one to the other. A city is not the country, and urban living has its own particular delights, but the roar of the expressway or the stench of overcrowded, airless rooms is not part of the delight. Neither are traffic jams, poor schools and lack of beauty. It is up to the physical planner to provide ways by which the opposing requirements of our time can be, if not reconciled, at least brought into some sane relation with each other.

Underlying these highfalutin notions are the everyday pres-sures of economics and politics. These pressures must be recognized and dealt with, or you are out of a job. But there is more than one way to skin a cat; and if you have an idea and don't tell anyone they may not recognize it and so perhaps will let you do it. Or maybe you can disguise it in such a welter of statistical tables that you can prove it to be desirable. After all, that is what statistics are for, and a good statistician is invaluable, particularly if he can talk fast. But seriously, half at least of the statistical work in planning isn't worth anything except to "prove" an obvious point and fortify an *a priori* conclusion. If you are really trying to plan for the future, statistical data of any kind, economic or physical or social are only a taking-off point. What you think of the future can only come from a feeling for trends, based on a knowledge of what is going on in the world of technology, and an intuitive understanding of people. . . .

I want to say just a few words about the day-to-day job of planning—the problems of zoning, of subdivision, of trying to preserve the integrity of the master plan. Most of the zoning and most of the subdivision regulations in the country are outmoded, and their interpretation has bogged down into either an unwieldy mass of amendments or a series of subterfuges, often dishonest. The situation is very much like that of building codes: new materials, new techniques, new concepts have made them obsolete. There has been a great drive for revision, for a swing to the so-called "performance code" which is more flexible but also requires more competent administration. Zoning and subdivision regulations likewise need rewriting, and for the same reasons; but if the rewriting is to be effective we must also revise the administrative procedures. The lay board of adjustment is quite incompetent to interpret a flexible zoning law, and the planning commissions of small towns and villages likewise are not able to do a sound job of dealing with subdividers without the help of a capable technician.

Aside from technical defects in much zoning, there has also been developing a lamentable trend towards using it as a device for economic segregation and to extend its power into the field of esthetic censorship. This is true not only of suburban areas, where it is most obvious, but also in larger cities, where it is not so apparent. I believe planners should do all they can to combat these trends as un-American and undemocratic. This will not be easy, because the idea of land-use segregation in its extreme form was a basic tenet in the early days of zoning, and now that the real-estate interests have latched on to it as a device for what they call the preservation of land values it will be very hard to stop the process. [Land-use segregation would confine each area of a city to one purpose only—such as commercial, residential, or industrial.—Ed.]

However, these and most of the other difficulties that confuse and depress us are part of the price we pay for planning in a free society. The conflict of opposing interests is the essence of a democracy. It is valuable, too, in keeping the planner humble.

I think that one of the most urgent problems we have to study is that of looking to a solution of the urban pattern. . . .

Now we come to a question of What is urban? Again, definitions will differ with opinions, but also again, there is no difficulty in agreeing that rural, suburban, and urban have perfectly understandable common connotations. There are border-line places, too, that are by common consent neither one nor the other. Mount Vernon, adjacent to New York, is neither urban nor suburban; I suspect Camden is the Philadelphia equivalent. That is because they are adjacent to a great urban center: remove them and they become urban, like Bridgeport, Connecticut, or Wilmington, Delaware. What I am getting at is that the idea of a city is quite understandable if indefinable. It involves, among other things, a high population density, a high degree of social anonymity with the concomitant of a very considerable freedom of action both moral and occupational, the stimulus of a variety of people, and the possibility of cultural improvement.

If you are going to have these things, I maintain you cannot plan them. They are of the essence of a city. All you can plan for is: first a traffic pattern; second, a concentration of population; third, a way by which a measure of quiet and safety can be obtained within the high concentration without interfering with the mobility and action of the population; and fourth, within such a framework complete liberty for the development of typical urban life and confusion.

I am not telling how to do it, I am posing the problem. I only know that the planner's ideal of complete segregation of land uses is absolutely the wrong answer for a city. People do not leave the farm to go to Podunk; if you try to make New York and Philadelphia an agglomeration of Podunks, you will happily fail. I think the neighborhood concept is nonsense. It is a return to the old idea of the political ward. Perhaps it has some meaning for the village, . . . for the habitations of the reluctant, the frustrated or the self satisfied. But it is most certainly not urban. Where it develops naturally, well and good—but its basis is entirely fortuitous, and unless it happens to have an ethnic base it is so fluid as to be meaningless. So don't plan neighborhoods—plan areas of action, of life, which means, and I say it again, areas which are unplanned except in the broadest sense, so that the urban pattern of confusion can develop as it will.

As you have by now gathered, I am a firm believer in a reasonable amount of confusion and the opportunity for freedom of action, no matter what. . . . Allow, in your planning, for the elbow room necessary to do otherwise than what you consider perfection, because you may be, and probably are, wrong in your assumptions as to what perfection is for the other fellow. It is a rather fine point that I am trying to make. Of course you must have convictions; but a conviction is quite easy to come by, and is not necessarily right because it is yours. Try to plan broadly, so that different ways of living can find their place in the framework you create. Actually, the best planning, like the best government, is that which is least planned and least governing. Logically, of course that would mean none of either; unfortunately, humans being what they are, that would mean chaos and anarchy. But there is an essential truth in the aphorism, and I would phrase that truth this way: When you plan, consider the other fellow.

WHERE CITY PLANNING STANDS TODAY [6]

The story of city planning begins with the ugliness, noise, and filth of the new industrial cities, their lack of fresh air and recreation space, the steady growth of their slums and the devastation of the surrounding countryside. All this was most obvious in nineteenth century England, and some of the early socialists, like Robert Owen, tried to find remedies for the situation. Owen proposed in 1820 the founding of groups of agricultural villages, with between 800 and 1,200 inhabitants each, which would combine "all the advantages that city and country residences now afford," and eliminate the "inconveniences and evils which necessarily attach to both those modes of society." Later socialists, however, did not pay much heed to this particular aspect of the Industrial Revolution; apparently, they expected the liquidation of capitalism to solve these problems automatically. . . .

Nor did any of the other political reform movements of the time show more than a mild interest in city planning. As a result, this new field of study could develop without arousing political passions or prejudices. But this also meant that it could not muster much popular support.

Ebenezer Howard, an Englishman, whose book *Tomorrow: A Peaceful Path to Real Reform,* appearing in 1898, marked the beginning of the modern city planning movement, was less concerned than the socialists with the social, economic, or political causes of urban misery. Frankly utopian, he combined certain ideas of his time in a specific and creative conception that has guided most of the thinking of city planners ever since. The garden city, or the notion of the balanced urban environment, was his original idea. Instead of letting industrial cities grow planlessly and depopulate the countryside, he proposed to build cities that would combine the social and cultural facilities of the city with the closeness to nature of the village. The "idiocy of rural life" and the slumminess of city life would both be obviated. "Town and country," wrote Howard, "must be

[6] From article by Frank Fisher, a New York businessman and economist. *Commentary.* 17:75-82. January 1954. Reprinted by permission.

married, and out of this union will spring a new life, a new hope, a new civilization."

The size of the garden city was to be limited; Howard conceived of a maximum population of about thirty thousand. However, the precise figures are less important than the underlying idea that there was an optimum size for a city, that—to quote Lewis Mumford—"it must be planned to the human scale and must have a definite size, form, boundary." As a permanent reserve, a green belt of open country, around each garden city, would serve to prevent unwanted growth and also provide opportunity for local food-raising. Common ownership of all the land would prevent speculation, bad land use, and excessive density of habitation. Finally, the garden city was to have a sound industrial basis so that its inhabitants could support themselves. Unlike the dormitory suburbs of our time—some of which have arrogated the name "garden city" to themselves—it was to be based not only on a balance between town and country, but also between home, industry, and market; and between political, social, and recreational functions.

Six years after Howard's book appeared, the first garden city, Letchworth, was built in England by a specially organized association of Howard's supporters who were willing to invest their money in a new experiment with expectation of very limited financial returns. Letchworth was followed by a few similar projects in England, Holland, Germany, and the United States (where Radburn, New Jersey, embodied some of the same principles). The main practical difficulty was the inability of these projects to attract industries for the employment of their inhabitants; it is only the development of electric power and the automobile since then that has made decentralized light industries possible and attractive. The first large-scale attempt anywhere to carry out Howard's ideas had to wait forty years, for the British New Towns Act of 1946, which authorized the Minister of Town and Country Planning to establish development corporations for the planning and building of new towns in designated areas. Many of the projects started under this act are in the Greater London area, and constitute an attempt to contain the inevitable decentralization of that metropolis within a sensible pattern. [See "Britain's 'New Towns'" in Section IV, below.]. . .

What is human scale? Some planners, in order to obviate the vastness and lack of differentiation in metropolitan areas, try to arrive at a clearly definable "unit of urban life" that might serve as the cell of a reconstructed urban organism. Clarence Perry in 1929 proposed the "neighborhood unit," an area which would require and support an elementary school with from 1,000 to 1,200 pupils, and have a total population of from five to six thousand. Even if every family had a house to itself, it would be unnecessary for any child to walk more than half a mile to school. Such a neighborhood unit could support local shopping facilities, churches, a library, and a community center connected with the school. Through traffic would be routed outside the neighborhood, while the inner streets would serve only to give the residents access to their homes.

The neighborhood unit makes the rational planning of many community services possible. The bad distribution of schools and recreation facilities, for instance, which is caused by rapid population shifts and the consequent deterioration of areas, would be avoided by the stability of these planned residential neighborhoods. Their proponents also hope that these would restore neighborliness and participation in civic matters—which is somewhat debatable. The neighborhood is still part of the city, and will consist of persons from all walks of life and of all types of personality. Closer physical contact may reduce group prejudices among them but will not necessarily induce the warm friendliness of the small rural community. As William Slayton and Richard Dewey point out in a study of the "urbanite" in *The Future of Cities and Urban Redevelopment* . . . the spirit of community life seems to require a rather homogeneous population, similar in income, occupation, and education— which is why this spirit is found at times in low-income metropolitan housing projects or in upper-middle-class suburbs. But such homogeneous neighborhoods would eventually split the city into socially stratified areas and eliminate the present advantage of city life, which consists in the range and variety of the social contacts it makes possible.

The neighborhood unit as the basis for physical planning became as important an idea in city planning as the garden city, and other writers developed it further. In *Can Our Cities Survive?* (published by the International Congress for Modern Architecture—CIAM—in 1942 and edited by J. L. Sert), it was proposed that six to eight neighborhood units be grouped together to form a township containing in its center a high school and principal shopping facilities. Light industry would be sited nearby, but separated by open spaces from the residential areas proper. The city would consist of a number of townships grouped around a "civic center" containing cultural, sports, and administrative facilities. Heavy industry would be placed along the main transportation routes, which would bypass the city. In this manner the big city would not be condemned, but loosened up and transformed into a "regional city" that provided cultural and economic advantages without completely cutting man off from nature. This plan would also assure the stability and controlled growth of the place.

We may mention one more idea that has played a considerable part in the thinking of city planners. This is the "superblock." The superblock has already considerably influenced the actual practice of real estate developers. It is generally recognized that the old gridiron pattern according to which streets are laid out in many European and most American cities is wasteful. In the heydey of land speculation, it provided standard-sized lots for easy trading, apparently permitted the maximum utilization of land for building, and gave each house easy access to the street. The grid also had its effect on the type of construction characteristic of the older parts of our cities: impressive façades in front; dark and narrow interior courts in back; houses occupying the maximum percentage of land permitted by law; and tall buildings depriving their smaller neighbors of sun and air.

What convinced the real estate people that the gridiron should go was the fact that it actually wasted a lot of land in street space by making no distinction between local and through traffic. With superblocks, the land devoted to streets could be drastically reduced and be used for lawns and play space while still permitting a high degree of land utilization. A few interior streets and blind alleys could give access to the houses, which would no longer directly confront the noises and smells of busy thoroughfares, so that children could play safely out of doors. It should be emphasized, however, that superblocks by themselves do not answer all the city's problems. While superior to the old system, they may still preserve an undesirable density of habitation, even increase it; and when designed without imagination, the uniformity of a large-scale project of this kind is as oppressive as the endless mediocrity of gridiron streets.

The garden city, the neighborhood unit, and the superblock today all contribute to a single large idea; that the growth of cities *must* be planned, and *in toto*. The problem cannot be solved by separate plans for housing, traffic, schools, parks and recreation, without considering the activities of the city or region as a whole, including work, travel to and from work, education, shopping, amusement, and all other required services. Much of the work of the planning agencies set up by cities and districts today is devoted to an attempt to comprehend the entirety of a city's life in all its phases and deal with it by a master plan. Such a plan integrates many partial studies; an over-all estimate of likely population development, plans for industrial, business, and residential zones, traffic, schools, parks, water, and sewage-disposal plans. Obviously, such a complex undertaking needs constant revision to take account of new developments, and must be flexible from the outset. It has to be conceived not as a static plan but as a continuous planning process.

Though these theoretical solutions to the problems of urban life have been familiar for a considerable time, it must be admitted that their practical effect has been very limited. Our cities continue to decay in their centers while the uncontrolled sprawl of their suburbs fills the country with row upon row of mediocre and uniform houses. These are built without consideration of the strain they put on traffic and school facilities and they bring the cities they surround—deserted by a tax-paying resident population, but strangled by masses coming to work in it—even closer to bankruptcy. We do have decentralization now, but it is chaotic; we have garden cities, but instead of

being Howard's self-sustaining communities they are metropolitan parasites. Our country is experiencing the greatest building
boom of history, but our cities are still ugly and inefficient. . . .

The tremendous postwar building boom, surprisingly enough,
turned out to be the Waterloo of large-scale planning. Slum
clearance became less attractive to the slum landlords as the
postwar housing shortage again filled their houses at high rents;
and as real estate values rose again, the cost of condemning
property often became prohibitive. This meant that when slums
were cleared—as along the East River in Manhattan—costs
forced the redevelopment organizations, whether public or private, to insist on a density of habitation actually higher than
before. The introduction of the superblock and the construction
of tall buildings made it possible to do this while at the same
time devoting a much lower proportion of the land to the actual
buildings. But play and recreation space should be provided in
relation to the number of people housed, not in proportion to
the area covered. Overcrowding of community facilities and play
space, and unimaginative and monotonous architectural design,
have stamped these projects from the outset as the slums of
tomorrow. Moreover, they have not been integrated into the
rest of the city according to any over-all plan, as the new traffic
and school problems that have arisen in each neighborhood elo-
quently testify.

These disastrous practices in the rebuilding of urban centers
were matched by equally disastrous practices in the expansion of
the suburbs. Some of the residential suburbs that have sprung
up since the war rival the worst prewar speculative developments
in their uniform mediocrity—though most of them have at least
abandoned the rigid gridiron layout. The best of them are hy-
gienic dormitory towns, "garden cities" without industry, generally located on cheap land with poor transportation facilities
to the city and often completely without cultural facilities and
even schools. In most cases they are outside the jurisdiction of
the city and therefore not subject to guidance by a master plan,
even where such a plan exists.

The city planning movement now faces a unique situation.
On the one hand it is better equipped than ever, technologically,

to make a real contribution to the replanning of our cities. Nor
has it ever been in a better position institutionally: not only do
we now have planning bodies in many cities, but we have academic groups, such as the Urban Redevelopment Study of the
University of Chicago (which published the large volume *The
Future of Cities and Urban Redevelopment* . . .), and the Institute for Urban Land Use Studies of Columbia, that do excellent
work.

On the other hand, the million houses a year we have been
building since the end of the war have dispensed almost entirely
with such guidance as the planning movement could offer.
Where the influence of planning is evident in some respects—
such as the superblock and the replacement of the gridiron pattern by one following the natural contours of the terrain—we
still find certain serious and basic shortcomings. The vast amount
of building in America today, despite the real benefits planning
could offer, is still determined primarily by the economic interest
of the builders—which means that the interests, economic and
non-economic, of the rest of us are overlooked.

The problem of city planning today is, in the largest sense
of the term, a political one. How are the techniques of city planning to begin to operate so that we can enjoy the convenience,
variety, and interest which they are capable of bringing us? We
do not wish to imply that they offer salvation, and the only question is how to get people to reach out their hands for it. But
certainly, without some popular participation, the benefits city
planning can now offer will become illusory, and the frustrated
planners themselves are likely to turn—as some already have—to
grandiose visions divorced from actual needs. City planning
needs popular participation, not only in order to realize itself
practically but also because its aim is to serve people's wants,
and it must remain close to these if it is to fulfill itself. . . .

The suburb . . . has the same attraction for some city planners as for the many middle-class families who move to them,
and who are swayed partly by the real advantages of open space,
quiet, and cleanliness, and partly by the desire to establish their
status among people of similar standards. But the garden cities,
with or without industry, are nothing without the city core that

provides the essence of urban life in economic, social, and cultural opportunities. As Henry Churchill puts it in a brief pungent essay in *The Future of Cities and Urban Redevelopment,* the community of like-minded souls dwelling in well-ordered harmony amid neat community facilities is a dull utopia in which planners themselves would hate to live.

They forget that what makes them queasy is to many the only reason the city has for its existence, a vast confusion in the midst of which opportunity, honorable or other, offers its golden charms, and where melting away among other unknown failures is the solace for those who muff their chance.

No model community can replace the fascination of the city, which lures young people to it from all over the countryside. The massed power of stone and concrete, of machinery and the profit derived from it, may crush the human spirit and overwhelm the individual, but it also offers adventure and opportunity.

In order to find their direction, the planners will have to choose between values instead of trying to give all things to all men. They will have to keep in mind (as some already do) that relieving the present congestion of the cities is not enough: a collection of suburbs does not make a satisfactory city. The planners will have to think more deeply about the kind of life for which they are planning, and understand its ideals and its meaning, and the variety of forms in which it may express itself. To restore the city's fundamental meaning as a meeting place, without the weight of ugliness and disorder with which a century and a half of industrial growth has burdened it, should not mean the destruction of its essence as a concourse of different people, as opportunity for a great variety of experience through the exchange of ideas, goods, and services.

IV. PLANNING ACCOMPLISHMENTS

EDITOR'S INTRODUCTION

Throughout this volume, there are examples of the accomplishments of city planning—to meet a specific problem such as housing or urban transportation, or to channel the growth of an entire community into a healthy, efficient way of life. This section is devoted to a further group of specific instances of the results of community planning.

The first selection deals with the rehabilitation of a small but important portion of one borough of New York City, while the second describes the efforts toward an over-all remodeling of Chicago, the nation's second largest community. The next two selections take up achievements in small or middle-sized communities, where planning can be no less necessary and effective.

As examples of current planning developments outside the United States, the final two selections discuss the pioneering development of a community "federation" in Toronto, Canada, and the fruition, after decades of planning, of Britain's "New Towns."

These examples spell out the lessons of the previous section —that planning is a universal need which, properly executed, can produce worth-while, creative results in any community.

REBIRTH OF MORNINGSIDE HEIGHTS [1]

In New York and other major cities of the country, city planners and social scientists, faced with tough overpopulation and delinquency problems, are deeply worried about communities that are running down. Good neighborhoods become overcrowded; buildings show their age and maintenance slips; new groups pour in, competing for space, education, understanding;

[1] From "Rebirth of a Community," article by Gertrude Samuels, staff writer. New York *Times Magazine*. p26-7+. September 25, 1955. Reprinted by permission.

old groups, decent and devoted to the community, develop fears and flee to "safer" neighborhoods.

Perhaps more important than the physical blight itself is this blight's impact on human values. Social scientists note that in every community, the life or death of the area is traceable to the vision—or lack of vision—of its leaders. The real building blocks, they observe, are people; and whether a community lives and grows depends on whether people are being divided by worsening conditions, or held together by the cement of human relations.

These were some of the grim issues facing one New York [City] community—Morningside Heights—shortly after World War II. Situated in Manhattan and defined as the area from 108th to 125th streets and from Manhattan and Morningside avenues to the Hudson River, some 365 acres and 60,000 people, it was a uniquely cosmopolitan community with a split personality.

On an eminence of Manhattan, one side of the Heights rises sheer of the Hudson like a monument—a powerhouse of educational, medical and religious institutions that represent over forty nationalities. Here, where Washington had fought the British in the Battle of Harlem Heights, in magnificent buildings of Renaissance and Gothic influence, come men and women from the ends of the earth: to study in the halls and libraries of Columbia University and Barnard College; to live together in good will at International House; to train as ministers and rabbis at Union Theological Seminary and Jewish Theological Seminary; to study at Juilliard School of Music; to move in the solitude of the great Cathedral of St. John the Divine; and to work in the other institutions that grace the area, which is dominated by the Gothic colossus of Riverside Church. Set among curving lines of trees, and also bolted against interlopers, the "élite" side of Morningside Heights was then for the most part closed off like many another college community—"gown" against "town."

Physically, it could never escape its fate. It was in a decaying area. To the east where the Heights dipped sharply at Morningside Park, to the north where it descended to Manhattanville or "the Valley," the other side of the Heights was a spreading slum. The park was virtually off-bounds to students and faculty as "too dangerous." Poverty and delinquency were aggravated by the postwar influx of Puerto Rican newcomers crowding into an already overcrowded area.

In worry and alarm, the institutions, which previously had little touch with one another, much less with the rest of the community, turned for advice to an outside expert, Wilbur C. Munnecke, then vice president of the University of Chicago. Munnecke bluntly criticized their academic outlook as being not only against their own interests but lacking in democratic vision. He said that only "positive action" could remake the neighborhood. He urged Columbia, which held much of the land on the Heights, to think about pulling up the whole community.

Led by David Rockefeller . . . the institutions created a nonprofit corporation, called Morningside Heights, Inc., with a budget of $40,000 a year to "promote the improvement and redevelopment of Morningside Heights as an attractive residential, educational and cultural community." They chose as executive director Lawrence M. Orton, a member of New York's City Planning Commission since 1938, who could be depended on to think of human as well as building values.

In 1950, the writer visited the area and wrote of the plans and dreams of those attempting to reshape the community. Morningside Heights, Inc., then was mainly a fact-gathering agency. Its many studies showed that the large majority of people wanted to stay in the area; that much of "the Valley" was beyond redemption and would have to come down; that there was a shortage of schools. Basically, the people wanted to be happy where they were living; to have good schools for their children; to be safe on the streets.

Now five years later, you go back to see what came of the dreams. Has the blight been halted? How do the people feel about the future? Other communities, including one close to Morningside Heights, have been experimenting with housing projects and delinquency control, yet appear to be making no headway against deterioration. What was different about Morningside Heights' story?

Let Lawrence Orton tell it:

Bricks and mortar in new housing projects aren't enough to make over a community. To be sure, other neighborhoods are tearing down slums, and there's a great cry in many places about juvenile delinquency, and public education is a matter of universal concern. But in many neighborhoods the benefits are lost or minimized because each of the problems is tackled separately, and there is no unified community effort with everyone pulling together.

I often think that so many who are fighting juvenile delinquency, for example, are fighting forlorn battles. They're not bolstered by good housing, good schools, good recreation and broad leadership which give solid continuing support to the rounded program of all groups. This is what is happening up here. The efforts of all the different organizations and some new ones are geared to pyramid the benefits. You don't have this in many communities. You do have it today in ours.

What has been taking place is a complete recasting of the community. The changes in the physical plant have been stepped up by legislation; the human gains were wrought by the people themselves. The way has been hard and tortuous at times; there have been resistance and misunderstanding and hostility. "Urban renewal," the planners wryly observe, "can't be done overnight." But the achievements of the past five years—and the failures— make a dramatic balance sheet.

The Physical Plant

On the plus side some $60 million has been spent on or committed to both private and public housing in the Morningside-Manhattanville area—for a total of 4,209 family units, or some 15,000 individuals. A two-part plan was developed: The institutions created a real estate organization, the Morningside Heights Housing Corporation, and signed an agreement with New York City to build and finance a $12.5 million middle-income cooperative project; the Board of Estimate also approved plans for a $27 million low-income public housing project adjoining the cooperative.

Today, the old "La Salle Street slums" are completely demolished—some forty acres of antiquated rat traps wiped off the map. In their stead are rising the Morningside Gardens cooperative at an average down-payment of $3,200 and an average carrying charge of $21 per room per month; nearby, the General Grant Houses public project, to rent for an average of $9 per room per month. And, heartened by Morningside, Inc., and following surveys by that group, the City Housing Authority has condemned tenements to the north of the area, where Manhattanville Houses are to be built, starting next spring.

What is inspiring to many are the psychological and social insights that went into the redevelopment plans. For both Morningside Gardens and Grant Houses are to be twenty-one-story, skyscraper-type buildings—similar except for some balconies on the cooperative; both will be nonsegregated and "mixed up" housing in the best sense. With no barriers between the buildings—when landscaped, they will flow naturally into one another—the fairly comfortable and the poor, intellectuals, white-collar workers, truck drivers, porters, will be living side by side. The people who formerly lived on the site have priority on the new housing and buildings are rising rapidly. . . .

On the "plus" side is also the burgeoning of the institutions. Once, while President Eisenhower was president of Columbia, he looked out of his Low Library study to 116th Street which bisected the university, a dirty, hazardous street cluttered with cars, and commented wistfully, "Wouldn't it be great if this were one green stretch?" Today it is—the street is closed to traffic, with a lovely, flowing campus the result. And Columbia has plans for a new law building; an engineering center; a graduate resident hall, and an Institute of Arts and Sciences with lectures and concerts for the public.

Others likewise evidenced their faith in the community's future. St. Luke's Hospital built a new marble wing; Barnard unified and beautified its campus; Riverside Church plans a new parish house, and a block-long, seventeen-story headquarters of the National Council of the Churches of Christ is to rise at 119th Street and Riverside Drive on the Heights, as a center for Protestant denominations.

The Human Effort

On the "plus" side is the way Morningside Heights, Inc., became a kind of conscience for the whole community. On many fronts—housing, public safety, recreation and cooperative community planning—it developed teams of intellectuals, labor, civic and religious leaders to involve the institutions with one another and with the people of the community. For a long time the situation had been all downhill—juvenile crime, traced to Manhattanville, was increasing; so was the exodus to the suburbs. A Morningside Citizens Committee was created; hardworking individuals like Father George Barry Ford of Corpus Christi Church and Clyde Murray, director of the Manhattanville Community centers, and Puerto Rican leaders quietly persevered to interpret the changes to the people and fight the battle against public apathy. This is their harvest:

(1) *The people were helped:* Relocation of some five thousand families on the site was a delicate human problem. The shock of moving anywhere was hard for many poor families to accept. An extreme left-wing group called "Save Our Homes" had sprung up, charging that the intention of community leaders was to get Negroes and Puerto Ricans out of the neighborhood. "Save Our Homes" led demonstrations at City Hall. Its propaganda bitterly divided the community, many of whom could understand neither the language nor the issues. At first the Morningside Citizens failed dismally to reach the Spanish community—until Puerto Rican leaders created a West Side Spanish Committee which interpreted the aims of the community to the newcomers "at their own level, to give them a feeling of belonging."

Rumors were scotched when more than thirty civic groups, including trade unions, veterans associations and social agencies, gave their approval to the Morningside Gardens cooperative. A humane approach to relocation and new tenancy was assured by the hiring of a staff of former New York Housing Authority experts which kept careful records of every family; paid bonuses and expenses to families having to move; planned demolition gradually so as not to move people about blindly.

(2) *Newcomers will be helped.* Some fifteen thousand residents will be pouring into the new homes—some new, some former site tenants—and their integration is not being left to chance. The planners want to build a good community spirit among them. Recently, at a branch library, representatives of twenty-five religious, school and civic groups met to discuss "welcome" techniques and plan visits by volunteers. "We can make the residents aware," says Father Ford, his face alight with hope, "that not only is this a great time to be allied with this community but that it will be even better."

(3) *Property owners are cooperating.* The most tragic pockets of blight in the area are the privately owned buildings and the so-called residential hotels of transient occupancy and questionable pursuits. The lack of decent occupancy standards is the curse of the entire city; lacking such standards and helped along by the greed of some landlords, many buildings have steadily deteriorated in the area. Recently, some forty local landlords were brought together by Morningside Heights, Inc. They formed a Property Owners Association to encourage good housing standards and to explore the possibilities of financing building improvements.

(4) *Youth is being helped.* Paid experts from Teachers College have been working with teachers of Public School 125 to enrich their programs with play therapy and art and music guidance. From a sense of panic, there is also developing a broad sense of security in the community today; the crime incidence . . . dropped 40 per cent . . . [after] police patrols were added to the area [in January 1955].

Of vital importance is the evolution of the institutions as a social force. The Cathedral, whose guards had always warned youngsters off its grounds, has now thrown its gates open to play groups; it also boasts one of the city's most popular summer camp programs, supervised by the Young Men's Christian Association, with children recruited by the Citizens Committee. Columbia has opened its Baker Field uptown to the community's youngsters on weekends. Today, several teams of former street gangs play baseball there under the supervision of volunteers. . . .

The "minus" side of the balance sheet shows that the battle for a healthy community is far from won.

Father Time—obsolescence—is in there scrapping. In the past five years, whole tiers of blocks south of the institutions have slipped in the natural process of aging, but even more through overcrowding. There is the recognition that unless many of these buildings are depopulated, the improvements will never overtake the spreading blight.

As for schools, the two elementary schools and one junior high are inadequate; this deficiency is largely responsible for the departure of families. An outside expert has been hired to counsel the community on its school needs.

There has been inadequate planning for the "in-betweens" —those families not eligible for public housing, yet not comfortable enough to buy a cooperative. Many in this group will be off the site permanently—the lower middle-income group which can afford but $12 or $15 a room rent. Some consider this a definite loss to the community, though it is also observed that the planners had to work within the framework of existing legislation.

There is still a large area to explore in community relations. While many of the suspicions between the Heights and the Valley have been broken down, there are fears that the low-cost housing "will be slums in five years." As Anne Ruddy, principal of P. S. 125, puts it: "The people on the hill still have a long way to go to be sold on their responsibilities to the community and to the schools."

There is clearly much to be done in the years ahead. But the balance sheet for the past five years contains lessons for other communities facing similar problems:

To make any community over requires teamwork—the mobilizing of all the social, business, cultural forces.

Just as important is the mobilization of the people—for people can become a negative force, as they were for a time in Morningside Heights, unless they are made part of the program. Nor can people do the job alone: they must work with government, with school authorities, with law-enforcement agencies to effect neighborhood betterment.

Above all, a community needs trained leaders to be the "social engineers," to bring about the cooperation of private and public agencies that can revitalize a community. These are the people who realize that you can wipe out all the slums "and still not have a community" unless all are educated to live together on a friendly basis.

Father Ford gave point to this concept not long ago in another New York community. Well-to-do, civic-minded representatives were attending meetings on upper Park Avenue and their talk was bitter about deterioration and what the city authorities should be doing for them. Father Ford sat on the sidelines listening. Finally he was asked for his opinion.

"I've heard all the criticisms here against the city," he said, "because of its apparent or real neglect. I think it's generous of you to come together to discuss your community's needs. But did you ever stop to think that you might adopt the responsibility for your own neighborhood?" In the shocked silence that followed, he went on, "Because the criticism is really against yourselves rather than against the city. What you're not seeing is your own opportunity."

Morningside Heights saw its opportunity. In fact, it was—and continues to be—this vision which is bringing about its rebirth.

THE BATTLE FOR CHICAGO [2]

Right now the most exciting city in the United States is Chicago, Illinois. What is happening in Chicago amounts, in many ways, to a rebuilding of the city. Chicago has needed the rebuilding in the worst way; it is getting it in a big way.

There has been talk of this rebuilding job for many decades; there have been large and sensible plans for it, and public orations to celebrate the plans. There have also been, in recent years, fourteen city departments, boards, authorities, and commissions to speed the plans into action—not to mention a revolving procession of private planners and project-pushers.

[2] From article by Daniel Seligman, associate editor of *Fortune. Fortune.* 51: 116-26+. June 1955. Reprinted by special permission; copyright 1955 by Time Inc.

And now, quite suddenly as it seems, the long years of waiting have ended. All over the city there is a fury of blasting and leveling. And as the girders go up for the new overpasses, office buildings, factories, apartments, stores, and hospitals, even the most skeptical Chicagoan, hardened against mere rhetoric during decades of tub-thumping, must now conclude that the city means business.

This, in turn, is good news for more than the 3.75 million people of the nation's second city, for more than the 5.5 million people of metropolitan Chicago (five northeastern Illinois counties and one Indiana county, according to the Census Bureau). Just about every major United States city is confronting the problem of what is today called "urban renewal." Given the condition of Chicago, success there would suggest that no other case is hopeless.

Chicago built practically nothing during the 1930's. During World War II, Chicago did plenty of industrial building but this only accentuated the need for every other kind of building. Postwar prosperity intensified all the pressures on the city's services; at the same time the city's gamy politics seemed to guarantee that nothing would get done. As of 1950, Chicago was a desperately rundown city. It seemed the perfect case in point for those who argue that the big American city is a failure. Today, if Chicago has a point to make about United States cities, the point would be this: if Chicago can start rebuilding, what city cannot?

A start is just what Chicago has made. While the city is rebuilding spectacularly, it is also accumulating new blight week after week. The scope of the battle for Chicago may be gauged from one statistic: there are in Chicago today something like a million people living in areas that the city has decided are beyond saving, i.e., that will have to be razed and redeveloped. . . .

Chicago is . . . a city that takes city planning seriously; it is almost a staple of conversation. The city's Burnham Plan was one of the first to be adopted by any major city in the United States; moreover, its elements were dinned into the heads of Chicago school children for years. When many of Chicago's present business leaders were in the fifth or sixth grade, they

were confronted with *Wacker's Manual of the Plan of Chicago,*
an elementary-school text unlike any other in the United States,
and they dutifully learned the answers to such chapter-ending
questions as: "In the Plan of Chicago, what is of much promise
for the young people?"; "Why is the Plan of Chicago superior
to that of any other city, foreign or otherwise?"; and "What is
one of the great problems of the age and what is Chicago's
problem?"

Because they take planning so seriously, and because the
business community throws its weight around for the civic weal,
Chicagoans today are reasonably confident that their rebuilding
effort will continue apace. . . .

Among the visible evidences that Chicago is at last being
moved off dead center:

The tallest skyscraper put up in the United States in fifteen
years, a forty-one-story office building for Prudential Insurance,
has shouldered its way into the famous Michigan Avenue sky-
line. Four other big office buildings are either just completed
or soon to be started—this after twenty-one years without a
major structure going up in the business district.

The second largest airport in the United States (the first is
New York's Idlewild) will be added to Chicago's civic estate
when O'Hare Field is completed. It will be ten times the size
of the city's fiercely overcrowded Midway Airport, which now
handles 7.6 million passenger movements annually. . . .

Illinois Institute of Technology has completed about half
of its extraordinary $45-million plan to carve a 110-acre campus
out of a horrible slum area in south-central Chicago.

The first major application in the United States of the new
Eisenhower urban-renewal program is now under way in the
Hyde Park-Kenwood area of Chicago, where the University of
Chicago, working with the South East Chicago Commission (a
private group), is conducting a determined campaign to fight
off the slums. Some $6.5 million of Federal funds has been
committed for the clearance and redevelopment of forty-eight
acres in Hyde Park. [See "Urban Renewal Under the Housing
Act of 1954" in Section VI, below.]

A major assault on the parking problem, which so many cities are still just talking about, is well under way. A vast underground garage has been built in Grant Park, just east of the Loop [the heart of Chicago's business district], and five of nine multi-story garages planned for other areas of the city are now finished. All together, off-street space has already been provided for more than 10,000 cars in the business district alone.

The Congress Street Expressway, a $100-million, eight-lane artery running seven miles from the Loop to the western suburbs, is finally under construction, and a small section of it is actually in use. Five other expressways are also being built through and around the city; the most important of these links the main business district to O'Hare Field and the suburbs in the northeast.

After five years of speculation, negotiation, and recurrent trumpetings in the press, the Lake Meadows moderate-rent housing project in southeast Chicago, sponsored by the New York Life Insurance Company, was finally opened for large-scale occupancy [in 1954]. . . . The project, on 101 acres of erstwhile blight, will ultimately house more than 1,600 families. . . .

The Medical Center district, 305 acres on Chicago's West Side, is half completed. Already built: six hospitals, seven medical schools, two apartment buildings, at a cost of approximately $45 million.

Another medical development, the $37-million expansion of the Michael Reese Hospital area, is now about 25 per cent completed. The new development is on eighty acres, will include another hospital (1,000 beds), a medical school and research center, and six apartment buildings (1,000 units in all).

Residential construction is at its highest level since the boom of the 1920's. In the five years [between 1951 and 1955] . . . public and private housing together added 64,972 dwelling units to the city's total—a rate of building almost twice that of 1945-1949.

Beyond these very tangible portents of progress, there is the promise, in a variety of blueprints and committee reports, of another great thrust of building that could carry into the 1960's:

The Fort Dearborn project is a grandiose scheme for the demolition of a vast area on the near North Side, and the erection of a civic center and a housing development, all at a cost of something like $400 million. The exact boundaries of the area have changed several times since the initial proposal was made, but the plan still encompasses close to 130 acres. (New York's renowned Rockefeller Center is built on twelve acres.)

A series of proposals to take advantage of the St. Lawrence Seaway project would make Chicago a major port for transatlantic shipping and improve the link between the Great Lakes and the Mississippi Valley system. Included in the proposals: an expansion of the city's inland-waterway system, and the construction of a new port in Lake Calumet (at the southern end of the city).

A complete overhauling of the city's zoning ordinance (the first since 1923) is under way; . . . when it is finished, Chicago will have the best and most up-to-date zoning of any major United States city. . . .

A strikingly imaginative approach to the problem of the aging neighborhood shopping center—a problem that plagues all sizable United States cities—has been developed by Chicago's Plan Commission. This is called the "Perimeter Plan." . . . The plan envisages a "perimeter," i.e., a one-way traffic circle built around the older shopping centers. All passenger cars and trucks would be routed onto this circle; no private vehicles would be allowed inside it except en route to parking spaces. (Public buses would, however, go into the core of the shopping centers.) The streets inside the center could thus be narrowed or eliminated, and the space opened up for parking lots, arcades, pedestrian plazas, etc.

The State Street Promenade is another Plan Commission baby. The vision here is of six or more bridges (cost: about $50,000 each) to be built into a second-story "shoppers' promenade" connecting Marshall Field's to Goldblatt Brothers, and perhaps the latter to Sears, Roebuck. The promenade idea would also be feasible in other parts of the city, the commission thinks; in any case, something like it is necessary to relieve the crush of pedestrians, and to separate the latter from the drivers.

An eruption of private planning for the long-range future of the Loop came last year in a $32,500 contest sponsored by the Carson Pirie Scott and Company department store. The first prize ($20,000) went to a five-man team of architectural students whose vision of the Loop in A.D. 2054 included moving sidewalks, parking in one-story garages under offices, separate road systems for trucks and autos. Only one of the first-prize winners had ever been in Chicago.

These broad, long-range plans have been nicely complemented by a great deal of down-to-earth neighborhood planning by organizations working to protect their communities from Chicago's largest immediate problem: the continuing spread of the slums.

The battle for Chicago, it will be observed, is pretty much confined to the problem of renewing the city's physical properties. It might, of course, be said that Chicago, like other cities, is fighting an industrial and commercial battle, that it is recurrently engaged in efforts to expand its business and employment opportunities. But this sort of battle is one that the city has been winning consistently. Its economic performance in the postwar years has been astonishing. The city . . . [in 1954] had an industrial production of $17 billion—compared with $4.3 billion in 1939 and $8.7 billion in 1946.

To its familiar firsts as a railroad and meat-packing center, and as a manufacturer of electric machinery, the Chicago area in 1953 added leadership of the United States steel industry. Chicago's steel capacity is now about 2.5 million tons ahead of Pittsburgh's, and Chicago has been operating at a higher percentage of capacity than Pittsburgh—the figures last year were 76.5 and 72.3 per cent, respectively.

Since the end of World War II, more than five hundred factories have been built in the Chicago area—a figure that more than doubles the industrial building record of any other metropolitan area. About 20,000 production jobs are created annually in the Chicago area. All together, there are now more than a million manufacturing jobs in the area (more than 600,000 in durable goods).

The industrial boom has, of course, performed miracles for the standard of living of Chicagoans. And ultimately it is this fabulous economy that is providing the wherewithal for the assault on decay.   Yet to some extent this economy is itself the source of the problem: it steadily gobbles up the city's resources (e.g., land, roads) and lures thousands annually into a city that has too few places to house them.

While the area's heavy industry has been thriving, the retail merchants in the Loop have had formidable difficulties in preserving their business.   In recent years there have been two problems confronting this business: first, the flight of many middle-income Chicagoans to the suburbs, with the subsequent transfer of their trade to the new, outlying shopping centers; and second, the chronic traffic congestion in the Loop itself.

The initiative in breaking the traffic jam came from local businessmen.   In 1949 the State Street Council and the Association of Commerce and Industry proposed that the city concern itself about the loss of retail trade to the outlying shopping centers.   Moreover, the two groups spent some $60,000 researching the problem.   At the end of 1950 further studies were made by a group of investment-banking firms.   The latter then proposed to the city a $50-million program (since raised to $100 million) for off-street parking. . . .

In the end, the battle for Chicago will be lost or won on the housing front.   The city's ability to renew its residential building, and above all to stop and reverse the spread of the slums, will be crucial.

Chicago's housing and redevelopment program is headed by a businessman, James C. Downs, Jr., who has the imposing title of Housing and Redevelopment Coordinator.   This title carries no statutory backing; it was devised in 1947 by Mayor Kennelly, who felt that someone was needed to knock together the heads of the proliferating city authorities in the housing and redevelopment field.   Downs has held the position since 1952 and has filled it admirably, in large measure because he has had the complete backing of the Mayor's office. . . .

With a few notable exceptions (e.g., Lake Meadows), private housing has had little to do with the battles against the slums; it has been confined largely to luxury-apartment building and single-family homes in the newer suburban areas.   The city's most conspicuous weapon, of course, has been public housing. From 1945 to 1953 the Housing Authority built 5,471 living units. . . . [In 1954] alone it built 1,820—the rate has been speeding up.

But in the long run, public housing would prove a slender reed for the city to lean on. For the city's capacity to build is limited by its capacity to relocate the families who live in the slum areas being torn down. There is a point, the Plan Commission believes, at which slum clearance for public housing (or for any purpose, actually) becomes self-defeating; the displaced families are forced to crowd into other declining neighborhoods, and so they create new slums as rapidly as the old ones are torn down. The city believes that its capacity to relocate slum dwellers is not likely to pass 7,000 families a year in the near future.

Thus the stress of Chicago's city and private planners has been increasingly on *conservation*—i.e., on slum prevention. To assist in its conservation fight, the city has a new Urban Community Conservation Act, which grants to a five-man board extraordinary powers to condemn even non-slum dwellings. . . .

An important conservation movement has got under way without waiting for the new board to act. The movement has been initiated jointly by community organizations, working to preserve their own residential areas from the blight, and by the city.

There are now thirty-six community conservation groups in Chicago; their jurisdictions cover half the city geographically and two-thirds of its population. Of the thirty-six, about eighteen or nineteen now have permanent staffs and offices. All of them rely, in varying degree, upon the Office of the Coordinator and on the Plan Commission for inspiration, technical assistance, and political guidance. There is no city money behind any of these community groups, however; their support comes largely from business contributors, some of whom act as charitable dogooders, but most of whom have an economic interest in warding off the blight.

These community conservation organizations have been battling the blight in varying ways. In a few cases, they are sponsoring limited redevelopment projects to extirpate pockets of blight before these spread. Other groups are primarily interested in paint-up campaigns. The major anti-slum activity of most organizations, however, seems to be the exertion of continual pressure on municipal agencies to carry out the police, sanitation, and inspection functions the law provides. Since the city, in turn, exerts some pressure on these organizations to get out there and fight for their neighborhoods, conservation in Chicago sometimes seems a rather circular operation. . . .

Unless Chicago is to shrink in stature, someone has to come in and do the work; and so long as the city is short of decent housing, there will be a tendency to overcrowding i.e., to slum formation. In the end, the slum problem can be solved, but it will be a long, hard war, and it will have to be fought on at least two fronts: First, the city will have to rebuild just as fast as it can relocate slum dwellers. And second, the city's (and country's) economy will have to keep pushing up living standards, until those last million Chicagoans can *afford* decent housing.

Chicago has almost always been growing "too fast." Except in the 1930's, its robust economy has been expanding relentlessly. Its industry's chronic need for land and labor has made mere living in the city a recurrent tribulation.

The fact that growth, and not stagnation, has been at the heart of the city's building difficulties has always been a source of considerable solace to Chicagoans. It doubtless accounts for their invincible civic optimism during the bleak-do-nothing years. Now that the city has finally been pushed off dead center, this optimistic temper will help keep up the momentum. Chicago's prospects have not looked so happy in a long while.

ACHIEVEMENTS IN A SMALL COMMUNITY [3]

Cleveland, the county seat of White County, is located in a beautiful valley of the Blue Ridge mountains of northeast Georgia. The city had a 1950 population of less than 600 persons and a low average per capita income. . . .

[3] From "How a Small City Benefits from Planning," article by L. R. Cooper, chairman, Planning Commission, Cleveland and White County, Georgia, *American City.* 69:103-4. October 1954. Reprinted by permission.

[The story of Cleveland] demonstrates, in the first place, that effective and enterprising community leadership may come from elderly citizens. This has special significance at a time when our population is aging. . . .

In its early years, Cleveland showed much promise. It had a bank, a railroad, two prospering resort hotels, and excellent shops and stores. But the community became a victim of changing times.

By 1944 the bank had failed, the two resort hotels had burned down and had not been replaced, and the railroad had discontinued its services and removed its tracks. The town had grown shabby and unattractive. Once a month the Mayor passed the hat to obtain enough money to pay the city's electricity bill. . . .

The required community leadership was provided by an elderly citizen, . . . Henry D. Wiley, aged 85, who in the spring of 1945 brought the citizens together and inspired them to improve their community.

What happened under Mr. Wiley's leadership makes [another] . . . significant demonstration—namely, that an enterprising and determined community can literally pull itself up economically by its bootstraps. With no visible financial resources, the city built a public water-supply and sewerage system, paved the town square, built sidewalks, and installed a much-needed street-lighting system.

These accomplishments were so outstanding that Cleveland was awarded first place in the 1948 Champion Home Town Contest sponsored by the Georgia Power Company. In 1953, Cleveland won first place again in this same contest—the only city in the state that has twice won a first-place award.

The developments that took place between 1948 and 1954 continue the demonstration of economic achievement and add two other demonstrations of significance.

The first of these is a demonstration of democracy in action. In 1952, a national zipper manufacturer was seeking a location for a new plant in north Georgia. The choices had been narrowed to two cities.

In the one city, the political leaders assured the manufacturer that they wanted the plant and would cooperate in making its operation there a success. In the other city—Cleveland—the political leaders suggested that they be permitted to bring the citizens together so that they might meet with the plant representatives, learn about the plant, reach their own conclusions, and speak for themselves. This was done.

The solid evidence of widespread citizen interest and support disclosed at this meeting and the democratic methods of decision-making employed in that community were important considerations in the decision to locate the zipper plant in Cleveland.

What happened next demonstrates that no city is too small to plan for the future development or to benefit from that planning.

At the time the decision was made to locate the zipper plant in Cleveland, the citizens realized that the new industry would attract many new people and would bring problems with which the city was not prepared to cope. The citizens called on the Georgia Power Company for advice on how to meet these problems.

The power company suggested that the community needed to plan for the changes that were coming and recommended that help be sought from the city planning and architectural students of Georgia Institute of Technology. This was done. Arrangements were made for the students to be given the planning of Cleveland as class problems. No charges were made for the work of the students, but the city paid their travel and subsistence expenses.

The first recommendation of the Graduate City Planning students was that the city and county seek a special state enabling act that would authorize the establishment of a joint city-county planning commission and would grant to both the city and the county the power to zone, to control land subdivision development, and to protect the bed of mapped streets. The students prepared the suggested enabling legislation; it was promptly enacted by the state legislature, and the city and county established a joint Planning Commission.

Working closely with the newly established planning commission, the Graduate City Planning students assembled basic information about the city and county, made a survey of existing land uses and a proposed land-use plan for the city and the surrounding urbanized area.

Subsequently, the students prepared a suggested zoning ordinance for this same area. The ordinance has been reviewed by the Planning Commission, and was adopted by the Cleveland City Council on August 3, 1954.

The city square presented a special problem. It contains, in the center, a brick Georgian Colonial courthouse that is in need of extensive rehabilitation and is limited in size for its required functions. The townspeople were divided on the question of whether to preserve the courthouse (either as a courthouse or for some other function) or to remove it and build a new, modern courthouse at another location.

A major north-south state highway passes through the square and a lesser east-west highway crosses its southern edge. The square is badly congested and presents serious traffic hazards as a result of the highway traffic movements and of large numbers of parked cars. For the most part the square is now bordered by unattractive wooden frame structures or low masonry buildings.

At this point in the city planning studies, a group of architectural students were brought in. They organized themselves into five teams to prepare alternative preliminary plans and models for the redevelopment of the square—some retaining the existing courthouse and others removing it, some retaining the highways in their present location, others wholly or partially bypassing the square. The property owners on the square had agreed to defer new construction until the preliminary plans were completed and the community had decided which one it liked best. They agreed that they would thereafter construct any new buildings on the square in conformity with the accepted plan and, as rapidly as possible, bring the buildings that are retained into conformity with the general scheme through reconstruction of the building fronts and other devices. The services of professional architects would, of course, be required for this work.

When the planning studies and the preliminary architectural plans and models were completed, the city, the county, and the Georgia Power Company joined in the sponsorship of a "City Planning Picnic" for the presentation of the work of the students. Every resident of the city and county was invited to bring a picnic dinner adequate for his own family and several other persons.

Distinguished visitors from elsewhere in the state and representatives of the press were invited. More than eight hundred persons attended the picnic and the following session in the school auditorium at which the students of Georgia Institute of Technology presented their findings and recommendations to the community.

The citizens of Cleveland, on that occasion, expressed their intent to carry out the recommendations of the studies in the years ahead and to make Cleveland and White County an ever better place in which to live.

As a next step, the plans and models for the redesign of the courthouse square were placed on exhibition in specially prepared cases in the courthouse. Ballots and a ballot box were placed nearby. Citizens were invited to study the plans and models and to vote for the one they liked best. The winning design was one that retained the courthouse.

Since the completion of the studies and their presentation, a second new industry—a woolen mill—has selected Cleveland as its location. The prosperity that has come to the town, as a result of these new industries and the community foresight that made their location in Cleveland possible, is evidenced in part by the million dollars now on deposit in the local bank but, even more importantly to the people, by the increasing numbers of their sons and daughters who are finding employment opportunities and pleasant living conditions in Cleveland and White County and are making their permanent home here.

COMMUNITY PROGRESS
THROUGH PLANNING FOR INDUSTRY [4]

Wooing industry still pays big dividends both to industry and to the community.

That's what the many United States communities say which have spruced up and actively courted new industry to come to their town. . . .

The movement, for that's what it is, to bring new industry and life to a community is called area development. A city or town doesn't have to be on the skids to feel the need for such development. Cleveland [Ohio], after . . . [the war], was a bustling metalworking town with no depression in sight. But a lot of former defense-work manufacturing space was due to be open. So, the Cleveland Electric Illuminating Company began what has become its "Best Location in the Nation" campaign. . . . [The company cited as results of this campaign the addition of about $1.8 billion in new plants and expansion from the end of World War II to 1953, with further expansion and improvement continuing at the same pace.]

Other towns, like Wilkes-Barre, Pennsylvania, have found themselves a one-industry town, and that industry declining. In Wilkes-Barre it was the anthracite coal mining industry. . . .

The Greater Wilkes-Barre Industrial Development Fund was formed in 1940 to help counteract the job trend. . . . In 1952 "Operation Jobs" was begun under leadership of a Committee of 100. Its efforts have brought fourteen new industries to greater Wilkes-Barre and twelve established firms have expanded within eighteen months.

How did they do it? The Committee of 100 raised $727,000 in free, unrestricted contributions for industrial development purposes. Vocational training facilities are being expanded to provide a pool of skilled workers. A choice 1300-acre tract is being developed into industrial sites. All segments of Wilkes-Barre have been enlisted in a drive to create a favorable atmosphere for industrial growth.

[4] From "Area Development Puts the Welcome Mat out for Industry," article. *Steel.* 133:66-7. September 14, 1953. Reprinted by permission.

The key to the situation is: Favorable conditions already existed there or the possibilities were evident. Wilkes-Barre simply put its best foot forward.

Outstanding example of grass-roots area development spreading over a large section of the country exists in New England. Each of the six states has a commercial or industrial development commission. From these grow community credit organizations, survey commissions and local city and town industrial development committees. Within this framework and cooperating closely are the railroads, power companies and other public utilities, chambers of commerce, New England Council and banks.

Local volunteers, under the direction of the State Planning and Development Commission, rang doorbells in Newport, New Hampshire, to uncover the exact size and composition of the town's workforce. They found Newport had a total available workforce of 480 of which 210 were unemployed. Of the 210, eighty-five had work skills of some kind. Newport considers this survey an important tool in cutting itself a slice of the new industry coming to New England. Newport people saw it work when nearby Hillsboro, New Hampshire, got the sleek, new $160,000 plant of Comfort Slipper Corporation. Hillsboro had to hump to assess its 2200 population for the available labor force. Newport is better prepared.

Many other towns and areas have put on similar campaigns— Detroit, Birmingham, Los Angeles—and each can point to concrete and encouraging results. Industry, they found, likes to be wanted. State-wide campaigns do not seem to pack the same punch as these local efforts. . . .

Industry men like to see a town stretch out the welcome mat for them. In fact, local groups often help answer critical questions which finally decide whether a manufacturer will build or not build in their community. Ford Motor Company says, in reference to its move into the Cleveland area, "We were very well pleased with the cooperative attitude of groups in Cleveland as we have been with groups in other areas of the country. We always want to be certain that our appearance in a community will not aggravate a lot of domestic problems."

So successful have been these local campaigns in providing suitable plant sites and a favorable atmosphere that some communities have gone too far, perhaps, to make themselves attractive. In those areas, industrial investment funds for building and equipment are underwritten by municipal or county governments. Usually such schemes arise where local conditions are not favorable for new industry under existing conditions. That twists a basic tenet of the area development movement. This is not an effort to sell a refrigerator to an Eskimo. This is a drive by local areas to discover and brush up their real advantages and resources and make them available to new businesses.

Such local communities are acting on their belief that United States industry is going to continue to grow. They're doing all they can to make themselves as attractive as possible to this new growth. And it's paying off.

TORONTO: EXPERIMENT IN FEDERATION [5]

[Since 1953] the city of Toronto and the twelve townships around it have been able to claim a unique possession—a form of government different from any other in North America. . . .

Toronto's plan of local federation may be unique on this side of the Atlantic (actually, the closest thing to it anywhere is the London county arrangement in England). But the problems it seeks to solve—problems that spring from the tremendous growth of the suburbs in the age of the automobile and the shorter work week—are common to practically every big metropolitan area.

The shift in living that has made the urban worker a suburban dweller has, in fact, made suburb and city into one continuous community. Yet the old political lines of the independent municipalities persist, blocking planning, development, and government of the community as a whole. At best, this produces a piecemeal approach to common problems; at worst, it results in grave inequalities stemming from varying needs for

[5] From "City-Suburb Federation: How Good an Answer Is It?" article. *Business Week*. p 64-6+. January 22, 1955. Reprinted by permission.

services and varying tax capacities within the towns to provide them.

As yet, no United States city has taken up Toronto's scheme of municipal federation to solve these problems, although attempts at federation go back as far as 1916. Federation, however, is simply one of many ways for achieving area government where annexation is impossible. In the United States, it may well be that some other device—the use of authorities or the transfer to the county of certain municipal functions—may prove a more acceptable way to achieve the same ends. Miami, for instance [recently] revived a proposal . . . to create area government through a strengthened county setup. But whatever course United States cities take, they are sure to be guided by Toronto's experience.

The Municipality of Metropolitan Toronto, which came into being on April 15, 1953, and began to function at the start of 1954, is actually a political compromise. It represents a concession by the City of Toronto, which wanted to amalgamate the suburbs and city into one, and by the twelve suburbs that doggedly insisted on holding onto some of their local powers.

From 1835, when it was incorporated, until 1914, Toronto provided for expanding population by annexations—growing from 10,356 acres to 25,000 acres. But in the forty years that followed the start of World War I, it annexed only 205 acres; strong opposition within the city kept it from gobbling up any big new areas.

The upshot was that Toronto's population changed hardly at all; in 1931, it was 627,231, little different from today. Meantime, the suburbs boomed around it—breeding bigger problems each year. Only Toronto, New Toronto, and Leaside had more than half of their total assessment in more profitable, nonresidential property. With little industry and commercial land to tax, the others faced a constant pinch in providing services for their growing population. Borrowing proved a poor solution. Strapped by limited credit, the municipalities had to pay as much as 5.75 per cent for their money—more than they rightly could afford.

Inevitably, the suburbs that could not expand their services fast enough, simply stopped issuing new building permits. Or they confined them to higher-priced homes.

Finally, after years of agitation that something should be done, the tiny suburb of Mimico in 1947 asked that a city-suburb area be created for the joint administration of certain services. The City of Toronto countered by calling for amalgamation of the city and all twelve suburbs into one. These proposals went before the Ontario Municipal Board, a quasi-judicial body that controls the borrowing and zoning of all municipalities in Ontario and is responsible for settling disputes among them. The board threw out both plans, and without being asked for it submitted one of its own.

The existence of the Municipal Board—and the fact that its plan went before the legislative assembly with ministerial backing, rather than being put to the voters—explains to a great extent why federation succeeded in Ontario, where it has failed in the United States. The board's proposal, which was largely the thinking of its chairman, Lorne R. Cumming, passed the assembly with only one significant change. This is what it did:

The City of Toronto and the twelve municipalities around it were bound together in one corporation, creating a new level of government, the Municipality of Metropolitan Toronto. The reins to this federation were put in the hands of a twenty-five-man Metropolitan Council, made up of twelve representatives from Toronto, twelve from the suburbs, and one council-elected chairman. Council decisions were made binding on all the municipalities—except that each of them has the right of appeal to the Ontario Municipal Board.

These are the council's main powers:

Assessment. The Metropolitan Council has sole responsibility for assessing all taxable property in the area on a uniform basis. Tax collection is left in local hands, but each municipality must pay a proportionate share of the cost of the metropolitan government. The council has the power to issue debentures for its purposes and for local municipalities; all are based on the metropolitan area's credit at large, and all are a joint liability of the area and each municipality.

Water and sewage. The council has exclusive responsibility for supply and wholesale distribution of water; local councils retain powers to build local mains and fix retail rates. It has sole jurisdiction over the construction and maintenance of trunk sewer mains and sewage treatment plants.

Roads and transportation. The planning, building and maintenance of metropolitan highways are under the control of the council; local councils retain their powers over local streets. Mass transportation is to be a monopoly of a Toronto Transit Commission, reorganized under the metropolitan corporation.

Education. The Metropolitan Council finances capital expenditures for school sites, buildings, and equipment. From legislative grants and metropolitan school taxes levied on a uniform assessment throughout the area, it supplies to the local school boards part of the annual cost of education.

Housing, health and welfare, parks, and planning. The Metropolitan Corporation has all the powers of a municipality in the housing-redevelopment field. It is responsible for certain health and welfare services—old-age homes, hospitalization of the indigent—for establishing metropolitan parks, and for area planning and development.

Fire and police protection are left in local hands; so are health clinics, off-street parking, civil defense, and the licensing of workers and tradesmen, such as cab drivers and electrical contractors.

The council has already asked the provincial government for these extra powers, and some municipal experts feel that whether or not it gets them will prove the real test of the metropolitan operation.

Nevertheless, Toronto right now has gone far beyond most areas in setting up control of essential services on a regional basis. . . .

Within Toronto, there is still strong support for amalgamation—and opposition to the federation idea. The city complains that with 57 per cent of the people, it is paying 62 per cent of the cost of the government.

The most widespread complaint of the suburbs is against the Toronto Transit Commission, which when it took over four privately owned suburban lines . . . set up a zone system and changed schedules and routes. Commuters who found themselves paying higher fares and walking further to bus stops had little good to say about the arrangement.

The same sort of irritation shows up over rates for services, such as water, and over the cost of the operation. Where a suburb has a high industrial ratio, it is likely to feel that it can take care of itself. New Toronto, which had "everything it needed," considers it is putting "everything we have into a church poor box." Against this, of course, the have-not suburbs are delighted with the system.

BRITAIN'S "NEW TOWNS" [6]

In Great Britain today there is a new development of tremendous significance in urban planning. Fourteen New Towns, centers of diversified industry, are being built to absorb population from the big cities. Residents are moving in as fast as homes can be completed for them. These are not boom towns that have suddenly appeared because of oil strikes or atomic energy plants; they are the result of half a century of solid thinking, followed by diagnosis and public conviction, about the ills stemming from the unlimited expansion of the cities.

The towns, for which the Government has already appropriated nearly $500 million, are carefully designed for an ultimate population of from 40,000 to 80,000 each. Around each is a *permanent* greenbelt of forest, agricultural land, parks and golf courses. The greenbelt is essential for two reasons: it limits the ultimate growth of the towns to avoid the social defects and wastes in municipal plant common to the indefinitely growing city; and it also keeps the residents in reasonably close reach of the countryside.

No less striking than the physical plan is the success that is being achieved in balanced development of housing and industry, and in the solid beginnings of communities of mixed economic levels. Since the start in 1950, about 220 factories with

[6] Reprint of article entitled "New Way of Life in Britain's New Towns," by Albert Mayer, architect and community planner. New York *Times Magazine*. p26-7+. January 29, 1956. Reprinted by permission.

7.5 million square feet of floor space have been completed and put into operation in the New Towns, and a number of these have since expanded. Nearly 200,000 people now live in 55,000 new houses and apartments in the fourteen towns. These people are grouped in neighborhood units that are a far cry from the upper class dormitory suburb. They have happily exchanged the crowded daily two-hour journey to work and back for twenty minutes or so of walking or cycling.

This creative solution for urban ills is a revolution in thinking and action. The British have become convinced that the only remedy for the troubles that have grown increasingly serious with the expansion of their big cities is to stop that expansion and even cut back by moving people out of the cities. The comprehensive solution of New Towns, they believe, is the only way to eliminate crowded slums and curb traffic congestion and the excessive costs of operating bloated cities.

The planned development which has now flowered into the New Towns had its genesis fifty or more years ago. Behind it were the British love of the green countryside—and the sight of the blighting after-effects, in grimy, congested cities, of the Industrial Revolution. The movement was given a tremendous impulse by the Garden City plan proposed around the turn of the century by Ebenezer Howard in his famous book *Garden Cities of Tomorrow*. As time went on, the difficulties of doing the job brought realization of the necessity for more drastic land control and development under Government direction.

Then came three monumental reports—those of the Barlow Commission in 1940, and of the Scott Committee and the Uthwatt Committee in 1942—dealing with various aspects of redevelopment. These made a deep impression on Parliament and the public. The creation of the Ministry of Town and Country Planning in 1943 was followed by the New Towns Act of 1946 and further legislation in 1947. Thus the legal, financial and administrative bases for the program were laid.

To attain its objectives and to keep people and industries from arbitrarily exploding into an unprepared countryside, the Government created a network of land-planning mechanisms covering all areas of the country. These can control and direct growth. They can, for example, prevent, if necessary, golf clubs or farmers near highways from selling out to builders and ribbon developments.

Another conclusion was reached. It is that the movement of industry must be subject to public authority. Industry is not told where to go, but through a licensing system it is told where it *cannot* go. Under this system, if an industry in London, for instance, wishes to expand by more than 5,000 square feet of space it must have a license from the Board of Trade—which can refuse the license unless the manufacturer is willing to move to one of the New Towns or to a depressed industrial area that is being redeveloped.

To carry out its program the Government set up Development Corporations for each New Town. These are made up of private citizens and are responsible to the Government. They are quasi-independent like our Port Authorities, but all their funds come from the Treasury, and there is an annual accounting and report to Parliament. The Corporations plan and develop the towns, building the bulk of the housing—which is public housing, subsidized, as elsewhere in England, to be within the means of the laboring and lower middle classes. There is, however, some housing for the middle- and upper-income groups. This is being developed by private builders.

The Corporations also build and own the shops and much of the smaller factory space, and derive nearly all their income from renting these. (This has worked well: as one index of effectiveness, the Corporations are earning around 6 per cent, after amortization of the funds lent by Government.) Most of the larger factories are built and owned by the industries themselves, but the Corporations have set careful criteria for the selection of factories to provide varied types of employment, competitors in the same field, and light industries where women can find work. Thus there is freedom of choice, so important to both labor and industry.

To examine the actual results of the program, consider the two towns that have made the greatest progress to date. They are Harlow and Crawley, both in the London orbit, about thirty miles out. Harlow has a population of 24,000 in 7,000 homes.

There are eight schools and fifty-nine factories with a total of
1.5 million square feet of floor space. Crawley has 5,000 new
homes housing 18,000 people and fourteen schools, fifty-two
factories and some eighty shops.

It is easy for the visitor to see that the advantages sought in
the New Towns are being achieved. The people live in intimate
proximity to nature as well as to their work, schools and shops.
The towns are divided into large neighborhoods, each with its
community and shopping center, playing fields and churches.
These neighborhoods will ultimately have populations varying
from 10,000 to 20,000 each when the towns are completed.
There are also sub-neighborhoods, the intimate social nuclei of
the towns, with five or six shops and a pub.

Major traffic streets run between neighborhoods, but outside
rather than through them. Pedestrians and motor traffic are in
general insulated from each other, and there are separate cycle-
ways. Careful planning has achieved not only attractive neighborhood schools and excellent house groupings but also a road
pattern that protects children from traffic dangers. Here one
feels with relief the lessened traffic density and hubbub.

Because balance has been achieved between population and
available jobs, and in equating jobs with people's skills, there is
little commuting; 90 per cent of the workers in Crawley came
out with their factories. Because of the good relation between
living and working areas, there is much less need for motor cars
and buses. Here, the automobile has truly become a pleasure car.

All this seems to have added up, so far at least, to a happier
population. Industrialists who formerly operated in London have
commented on the lower rate of absenteeism in the New Towns.
Less than 4 per cent of the people who moved into Crawley have
since moved away—a really remarkable showing, especially in
view of the rugged early conditions usual in all new developments. This is in spite, too, of the uprooting—albeit voluntary
—of the Londoner from his lifelong haunts and habits, and in
spite of the fact that rents are higher than he has been accus-
tomed to pay.

The pavement-bred Londoners are delighted with their New
Town gardens. In Crawley, where the front areas adjacent to

sidewalks were originally intended for municipal maintenance, the people's demand for gardens was so strong that regulations were changed accordingly. Building scars have quickly disappeared under the spade of the eager gardener.

There has been a lag in developing community and central facilities—which had to give precedence to housing and industry. Nevertheless, social life has made remarkable strides. In Crawley there are 248 clubs, societies, associations, sports groups and church organizations. They include the Floral Decoration Society, British Legion, Darby and Joan Club, Folk Dance Club, Recorded Music Society, National Association of Parents of Retarded Children, Rotary Club, Congregational Sisterhood, Teenagers' Club, United Nations Association, King's Lodge, Ancient Order of Druids, Over-Sixty Club, A. P. V. Athletic and Sports Club, and twenty-four labor unions.

In Harlow, the small "Common Room" has been developed as a modest and logical center for social life. Originally devised as a sort of stop-gap until larger facilities were ready, these rooms, which serve and are managed by some six hundred families each, have become convenient features. They are used for small local meetings, for children's clubs, parties, drama rehearsals, and celebrations. In a sense the Common Rooms serve as extensions of the functions and space of the present-day excessively compressed homes.

The New Towns are certainly not distinguished as yet for stimulating or challenging architecture, but these one or two-room centers are often striking architecturally. This perhaps is because they fulfill a new function.

The most handsome architectural and planning job in the New Towns has been done in the school and industrial areas. The industrial layout, marked by greenery and landscaping, has the appeal of orderliness. Individual factories have as common characteristics glassy modernity, sharp lines, and harmony. Everything seems to glisten, for power from gas and electricity here has replaced the old cities' soot-making coal and oil.

These industrial areas are bulwarks of private enterprise in its soundest tradition. Sectional factories designed by the corporations' own architects are built and rented in units as small as 2,000 square feet. These can be extended unit by unit for a rapidly growing small business. There are also intermediate units of 5,000 and 15,000 square feet, plus office space, for rent. The larger industries that have built for themselves have put much capital into construction; in Crawley some $15 million has been so invested.

It is too early to say to what extent those living in the New Towns will actually represent an economic cross-section, but the Crawley Development Corporation, for example, has already made appreciable progress in that direction. In both Crawley and Harlow more normal age distribution of the population is being sought by building special one-story houses for old people—and *not* in big groups, but in small clumps of three or four among families of younger age. In Harlow, too, an Art Trust has been established, and it is planned to have a group of artists move into town.

What application does the British precedent of the New Towns have for the United States?

In their performances to date the British New Towns promise to solve a number of difficult problems very similar to those we face in this country. We are still trying vainly to cope with our traffic problems with expensive clover-leafs and expressways and increased fares, and we are scurrying about to find new taxes to support our overgrown and inefficient cities. But we are still letting them grow, encouraging them to grow, while we despoil more and more countryside by unplanned "development."

The excessive costs of the overgrown city in terms, for example, of truck-and-man hours lost, in terms of bankrupt commuter railways and bus systems, in terms of increasing taxes to devise costly super-remedies that don't remedy, are inefficiencies in our productive system. And the monetary and social costs of uncontrolled industrial expansion into virgin land areas is terrific.

The British plan is a preview of what we could accomplish here. It is also a preview of what we have got to face in principle, in hard thinking, and finally, in law. The first thing that must be recognized is that city and regional planning are not just fancy gimmicks, but as essential to economical production and living as are the efficient factory lines we rightly pride ourselves upon.

Just as fascinating as the visible work of transforming theory into brick and mortar and steel and glass in Britain's New Towns is the legal, political and administrative pattern the British have so carefully constructed to make the transformation possible. Each element of the problem had first to be recognized, and then solved, against a tremendous complexity of inertia, and vested civic and economic interests. It was necessary to realize that the hopeless and bankrupting maze of traffic and transport could be dealt with only by far-reaching measures, that even the big step of effective city-metropolitan planning is not enough, but can be really effective in the long run only if there is a vital national policy against which the fragmentary projects can be measured and put together.

To accomplish what they are doing the British built an impressive edifice. It is an edifice created in law, in finance, in administration, in public opinion and in local acceptance by the most closely affected groups—the industries, the cities, and the countryside.

The various British controls may seem excessive or impossible in our individualistic culture. So they seemed to the British originally, not very many years ago. It may be noted that the first efforts at control of industrial locations in Britain were in connection with "depressed areas." Interestingly, not long ago the newspapers reported just such rumblings here. The Administration announced its ideas for a "domestic Point Four" effort to help the industrial economy of coal-mining areas in Pennsylvania and West Virginia and old textile areas in New England.

We have in this country an impressive amount of unrelated legislation in this field, some of which is drastic. It remains to put all this together and to interlace some big missing pieces. This isn't going to happen of itself. In Britain a combination of repeated frustrations in piecemeal efforts, of symptoms of crisis in big-city and abandoned areas, and a small, energetic group of far-sighted citizens did the necessary job. With these ingredients, it *could* happen here.

The major legislation in Britain was passed under the Labor Government, but the Conservative Government has pressed even further forward. In fact, under it there is a new law, the Towns Development Act, which permits large cities to take an additional step to reduce their excessive population by arranging with suitable small towns to enlarge themselves and become new planned towns of predetermined size. In this case the city must contribute financially, at so much per relocated family.

Though it is all but incredible in terms of our own civic psychology, London has gone at this enthusiastically and has already concluded agreements with five towns. In one of them, Bletchley, the resettlement is already under way. How this plan will work remains to be seen, but it does indicate what has been found to be necessary to solve the multiple troubles that continue to thwart the fantastically expensive individual-functional cures.

Thus, a new epoch has opened in Britain. Visitors come from all over the world to observe the New Towns. The town of Crawley has kept a record: visits by 770 foreigners; but only twenty-one of these came from the United States, and of these, seventeen were architectural students. Yet America can profit by this new concept more than most other nations.

In the last few years our country has arranged for efficiency teams from many nations to come here to study our industrial methods. In turn, we should send efficiency teams of administrators, city officials, industrialists and important public men to study the British New Towns. They would have a rewarding experience.

V. THE CITY SPREADS OUT

EDITOR'S INTRODUCTION

The past decade in particular has witnessed a spectacular new trend in American home-life—the growth of the suburbs, spreading with brush-fire speed. While suburban living is not new to the United States, the extent to which it has developed since World War II overwhelms all previous movement outward from the city.

Responsible for this has been the fact that ownership of one or more automobiles is now a commonplace in every American family above the lowest economic scale. In addition the ability and desire for home ownership now extends to families in all walks of life, beginning with the blue-collar factory worker.

Virtually all this growth, however, has had the effect of extending the influence of already existing metropolitan centers—New York, Chicago, San Francisco, and Los Angeles in particular. Thus the planning problem for these suburban areas is twofold: (1) planning the suburban area itself—and often in the light of an entire community springing up within a period of months; and (2) over-all planning of the entire metropolitan area, attempting to fit the new "fringes" into existing patterns.

The post-World War II changes effected by the new suburbia are discussed in the first two selections of this section. The latter two selections take up the over-all problems and challenges presented to the new metropolis. The second of these, while prepared as a discussion of the San Francisco Bay area, has relevance to all similar areas throughout the nation.

SENSATIONAL GROWTH OF THE SUBURBS [1]

A period of sensational growth lies ahead for the city and suburban areas of this country. Suburban areas very often are

[1] From "Rush to Suburbs Just Starting." *United States News & World Report.* 40:37-40. March 2, 1956. Reprinted from *United States News & World Report,* an independent weekly news magazine published at Washington. Copyright 1956 United States News Publishing Corporation.

going to double the number of residents within twenty years. Nearly all of them expect to grow by a half or two thirds in this period of time.

These rather startling figures of expected expansion turn up from a [recent] survey of large cities . . . by the Economic Unit of *United States News & World Report*. These prospects are based on studies of local planning specialists who applied official estimates of the Census Bureau to their own communities.

Some surprising forecasts are turned up. The Miami area expects to triple its population between 1955 and 1975. Los Angeles will double its population and overtake Chicago as the nation's second-largest city. More people will be living just outside of New York than inside the city. Fastest growth is foreseen for the areas around Miami, Los Angeles, San Francisco-Oakland, Dallas, Oklahoma City. Slower growth is indicated for areas around New York, Chicago, Detroit, Boston, Pittsburgh, Cincinnati.

Cities themselves often are found to be at or near the saturation point in population. Boston and Pittsburgh expect no increase within the city limits in the next twenty years. Cleveland and Rochester, New York, expect to lose a few people. There's not much room for growth in New York, Detroit, St. Louis or Washington, D.C.

All city areas, however, look for sharp expansion in the suburbs. Suburban populations are expected by 1975 to exceed central-city populations in 14 of . . . 24 [major] areas. . . . The suburbs are expected to have at least double the population of the city areas of Los Angeles, Boston, San Francisco-Oakland, Pittsburgh and Washington, D.C.

Actually, almost all the increase in population over the next twenty years will consist of growth in cities and their suburbs. The Census Bureau projects a population increase of 63.3 million people from 1955 to 1975, assuming that births continue at the present high rate. Of this increase, 46.5 million will settle in or near cities. And of the 46.5 million new residents, 38.3 million, or more than 80 per cent, will find homes in the suburbs. The increase in city areas may be even greater than 46.5 million, since sizable new cities may develop by 1975.

The trend toward urban living that has been going on in the United States since 1800 is to continue. More than two thirds of the population now is classified by the Census Bureau as urban. By 1975, urban residents are expected to make up nearly three fourths of the total. . . .

Miami, for example, expects to pass the million mark by 1960 to become the largest metropolitan area in the South. That means the addition of more than 250,000 people in the next five years. Planners in the Miami area quite clearly expect the demand for new homes, shopping centers and other facilities to be as great in the years immediately ahead as in the years just past, regardless of what happens to building and business trends in other parts of the country. The Miami area also expects to continue to attract new industries and to become less dependent on the tourist business.

What's happening in Miami is being repeated, though on a somewhat smaller scale, in many other parts of the country. Los Angeles expects to add a million or more people to its area population in each five-year span from now until 1975. The San Francisco-Oakland area counts on a more rapid rate of growth in the years ahead than in the years since 1950. . . .

The Philadelphia area demonstrates what often happens to a growth pattern. United States Steel Corporation established a new works in this area and an entirely new city—Levittown— is growing near by. Planners in Detroit note that, since 1950, six new villages and cities have been established in the metropolitan region. They see no indication that this trend will change.

In the period ahead, not only are present suburbs expected to expand, but new ones are likely to be born in many areas. Beside a need for housing, this also means a demand for entirely new sewer-and-water systems, networks of utilities, school systems, parks and playgrounds, stores and service stations, hospitals and office buildings.

In Detroit, planners see the need to destroy quite a number of dwellings to make room for express highways and needed redevelopment projects. Those same problems are to arise in area after area as the shift to the suburbs gathers speed.

The growth of suburbs also means added problems of revenue for the central cities. In New York, for example, planners see a continued decline in the middle-class population and a rise in the lower-income groups. At the same time, suburban residents will put added pressure on transportation systems and other city services. New York, in brief, faces the prospect of increasing demands for services and a population less able to pay for it. That situation is more or less typical of all big cities.

This explains why more and more cities are resorting to tax policies that tap the pocketbooks of outside residents. Sales taxes and payroll taxes are two of the most popular measures. Some cities also impose occupancy taxes on hotel rooms and put special levies on restaurant meals. Others are increasing their franchise taxes on business firms operating in the city.

Suburban expansion also is promoting what amounts to a revolution in merchandising methods. Department stores in almost all cities are finding that they must establish branches in the suburbs to maintain their sales volume. Other merchants often find that suburban locations are more profitable than sites in the crowded central cities.

The nature as well as the extent of retail markets also is changing as a result of suburban growth. Suburbs usually consist largely of single-family homes, with lawns and gardens. That means a wider market for plants and shrubs, for lawn mowers, garden tractors, household tools. People also are inclined to dress more informally in the suburbs than in the cities, and their entertaining is more often done at home. That affects the demand for clothing, for furniture and home appliances.

The family car, which often was only a luxury in cities, is a necessity in the suburbs. That establishes a wider market for automobiles. The second car for the family also is quite likely to be regarded as a necessity in suburban areas. What this trend means for the automobile market can be seen in projections that forecast a suburban population of 83.4 million people in 1975, compared with 45.1 million today.

While the cities and suburbs are growing, the farm population is expected to decline, both proportionately and in actual numbers. The number of farm residents now is put at 22.2

million people—13.5 per cent of the total population. Twenty years from now, only 15.3 million people, a scant 6.8 per cent, are expected to be living on farms. Most of the people who leave farms can be expected to move into suburbs, or their farms may be turned into subdivisions by the expansion of suburbs.

The shift in population that lies ahead actually promises to have more effect on business volume and on new problems in government than population growth itself. Increase in the whole population is expected to come to 38 per cent in the twenty years ahead, but cities will grow by only 16 per cent while the suburbs expand by 85 per cent. The living pattern of the American people appears certain to be undergoing a basic change.

TROUBLE IN THE SUBURBS [2]

Among the folklore that has grown up around the mass movement of Americans from city to suburb since World War II, no story better illustrates the problems involved in so staggering a shift of population than the case of the ambulant expressway. The road in question, some fourteen miles long, was conceived by the highway engineers in 1948 to resolve a dilemma confronting Nassau County, Long Island. This venerable haven for commuters, east of the New York City line, was reeling under the impact of a housing boom. Its population had doubled since the war. With roughly 800,000 citizens attempting to drive along highways designed to accommodate 400,000, a fantastic traffic jam developed. Movement was possible down the axis of the Island, which extends from west to east. But those who traveled from north to south for shopping or business found the trip an abomination. Mousetrapped by red lights, they inched through constricted village streets, already crammed with trucks and loud with the noise of honking horns.

The sensible answer to this nuisance was a limited-access, six-lane expressway, down which motorists could whiz without let or hindrance. A route was surveyed to run from Roslyn, on the North Shore, to Freeport, on the South Shore, fifteen miles

[2] From Part I of a three-installment article by Hal Burton, author. *Saturday Evening Post.* 228:19-21+. September 17, 1955. Copyright 1955, Curtis Publishing Company. Reprinted by permission.

through the most densely populated section of the county. The idea was fine, but only in theory. As first laid out, the new road would have required five hundred houses to be torn down or moved. Many of the owners looked with favor on the idea of a substantial cash settlement for the inconvenience involved. By 1950, however, another 450 houses had gone up along the right of way, and hundreds more were abuilding. The newly arrived settlers emitted a piercing shriek; the politicians ran for cover; and a bill before the New York State Legislature to authorize the expressway died in committee. "By the time the debate was over, so much land had been subdivided that the whole idea was hopeless," said Sidney Shapiro, chief engineer for the Long Island State Park Commission, which supervised the planning.

Over the years that followed, the traffic situation grew steadily worse. One route after another was hopefully proposed; then glumly jettisoned as citizens' committees met angrily in mass meetings. New housing developments continued to pop up wherever the engineers found a feasible right of way. Finally, in 1955, the route was shifted five miles to the east. This, the planners agreed, was the absolute outer limit for an expressway of any earthly use.

It goes without saying that 375 new houses had already risen along this right of way—and that 375 new home-owners were emitting anguished protests. These, for a wonder, got them nowhere. Robert Moses, president of the Long Island State Park Commission, put his foot down. He insisted that the expressway must run from Oyster Bay southward to the village of Wantagh, on Great South Bay. The legislature passed a bill formalizing the route. Governor Averell Harriman signed it. Yet even now, as the bulldozers warm to their job and the surveyors set out their stakes, committees work hopefully on new routes that would send the expressway through somebody else's front lawn, not theirs.

The case of the ambulant expressway is only one example of the utter confusion to be found wherever people have moved to the suburbs, which is virtually everywhere in the United States. Since 1945, more than 10 million new homes have gone up outside the city limits of America. Long Island and Los Angeles are spectacular examples. But the same zestful, disorderly growth is common to cities such as Wichita, Kansas, with a population of only 160,000. The Bureau of the Census, hard put to keep up with the figures, estimates that the suburbs now harbor 30 million persons. This is nearly one fifth of the total population of the United States. . . .

As the suburbs grow, the problems grow with them. Too many people in too much of a hurry have created a massive municipal headache. Highways are inadequate and overloaded. ("The cars come by so close together that it takes me fifteen minutes to back out of my driveway," one despairing old-timer told me.) Village streets can't handle the traffic that crawls through, stopping every few feet. ("I'm going to move my store out to the edge of town," one merchant said. "My customers can't even get their cars near the curb.") Towns that were foresighted enough to build parking areas fifteen years ago now find them far too small. They are frantically buying new land or else providing it by tearing down old buildings at a premium price.

Bus lines, practically all of them in the red, are antiquated or inefficient. The railroads, stuck with commuter lines that lose money, are apt to provide slow service, with infrequent trains and outmoded equipment—though there are a few shining exceptions. No matter how many new schools are built, there are more than enough children to fill them. Double shifts are a commonplace, meaning that each child goes half a day and gets half an education. Water supplies often are inadequate: ("I use one large kettleful of water three times," said a housewife in Fairfax County, Virginia, twenty miles outside Washington, D.C. "Once to sterilize the baby's bottle, then to bathe the baby, and finally to wash the baby's diapers.") Sewage-disposal systems lag hopelessly under an overload, it seems, no matter how much new pipeline is laid.

Where the money will come from to set all these things right is everybody's guess and everybody's worry. The most concise evaluation of the situation comes from Max S. Wehrly, executive director of the Urban Land Institute, which specializes in the study of municipal problems. "The suburbs," he says, "are incapable of finally supporting all the services they want. Either

they will have to consolidate, to merge with the cities or to bring
in enough industrial plants to give them adequate tax revenues."
The stopgap answer, now widely in use, is to call on the county,
the state and the Federal Government for help. . . .

There are some examples to prove that a suburb can grow up
overnight and still emerge as an efficient working unit. One
such illustration is the village of Park Forest, a planned community in the cornfields thirty miles south of the Chicago Loop.
Until 1947 the three-thousand-acre site was occupied by eight
farms and a golf course. Illinois Central trains went through
without stopping. Then the land was sold to American Community Homes, a building and management corporation which drew
its inspiration from Levittown, Long Island, a pioneer project in
the field of low-cost housing. The first family moved in during
August 1948. By July 1950, Park Forest was a community of
24,000 persons occupying 6,200 homes and rental apartments.
Eventually it will house 35,000 persons. . . .

Designed for young people, the community has a median age
of thirty-two and an average of three small children per family.
Neighboring school districts were unable to carry the added load.
Park Forest itself was so newly incorporated as a village that it
had an inadequate bonding capacity for new school buildings.
. . . [The development corporation] therefore undertook a series
of generous steps. American Community Homes paid the tuition
and bus fare of children shipped off to nearby schools. A rental
apartment building across from the shopping center was set up
as a temporary schoolhouse. . . . [The developers] then put
$2 million of the funds of the corporation into a nonprofit cor-
poration which built four new elementary schools. Part of the
money was an outright gift; part was a loan, most of which was
paid back. In some cases, the fruits of this enlightened policy
were fairly spectacular. One prolific couple, occupying a ninety-
one-dollar-a-month rental apartment, had five children of school
age. For each of these, the corporation paid twenty dollars a
month to a nearby school district—or, in effect, a one-hundred-
dollar-a-month baby bonus. . . .

The young executives, salesmen, Army officers and college
instructors who inhabit Park Forest are, by and large, happy with

their lot. But there are some dissenters. "It's like an Army camp," said one ex-tenant, who moved back into a crowded Chicago apartment after several years of fresh air and green grass. "Everybody is the same age and has the same number of kids. Everybody runs for the bus at the same time and gets on the train at the same time. There are about sixty youngsters to the block, and they travel in packs. You never see an older person around. My wife and I felt like ciphers."

After a tour of Park Forest, I could see his point. The best efforts of architects and planners have not been able to obliterate the deadly sameness that comes when you build houses by the thousand to sell for $10,995 upward. This, however, is the way that fortunes are made in real estate. Park Forest was planned so shrewdly that the development corporation can make a profit, any time it chooses, by divesting itself of three thousand rental units and operating only the utilities and the shopping center.

In Park Forest, as almost everywhere, the most urgent problem revolves around commuting. Eight railroads of the Chicago area carry 297,000 commuters a day. The figure includes those going into the city in the morning and also those going home at night. With one exception, despite fare increases, the commuter lines are losing money by the bucketful. The Illinois Central, which serves Park Forest, ran a deficit of $2,475,000 on commuter service between 1949 and 1952. The Chicago and North Western Railroad, which claimed a loss on commuters of $3 million a year, attempted to solve the problem by curtailing service. This, in one case, proved to be the tocsin for a commuters' revolt.

The North Western was operating a 5:05 P.M. through train to Clinton, Iowa, which was utilized by commuters as far west as Geneva, Illinois, thirty-five miles from . . . [Chicago]. The Illinois Commerce Commission, which regulates passenger and freight service, was asked by the railroad for permission to drop the 5:05 to Clinton. At the same time, the North Western promised to substitute a new 5:05 running only as far as Geneva. Beyond that point, only thirty passengers a day rode the train.

"Oh, no," said the commuters, banding together in a protective association. "If you take off the five-oh-five to Clinton, how do we know that you'll keep your promise to put on a five-oh-five to Geneva? Maybe you'll just forget. How about giving us a written promise?"

The railroad somewhat huffily said that its promise to the commission was good enough. Anyway, it didn't intend to start making promises to special groups of customers. The reply produced an outburst. Out through the western suburbs commuters rose to arms. There were mass meetings on the North Western station platform in downtown Chicago, and reams of unfavorable publicity on the front pages of the Chicago papers. . . .

[But] the North Western went right ahead and discontinued the 5:05 to Clinton, replacing it with the 5:05 to Geneva.

Keeping the commuter happy is a technique mastered successfully by ony one major railroad, the Chicago, Burlington and Quincy, whose passengers truly love it. The Burlington carries 38,000 commuters in and out of Chicago each day. In 1949, hoping to cut its losses by attracting new customers, the railroad laid out $10 million to modernize suburban trains. Revenues rose, but not enough.

In 1952, the railroad notified its commuters that it must ask for a 27.5 per cent increase in fares. Instead of an angry uprising, there was silence from the customers. Not one of them sent a letter or protest to the Commerce Commission or showed up for its hearings, and the increase was approved. . . .

Harry C. Murphy, president of the Burlington, is pleased, but no longer astonished, by this atmosphere of sweet reasonableness. "We couldn't get out of this commuter business," he remarked recently. "We've been in it since the 1870's. So we thought we might just as well try to provide a service that would make the passengers happy. As a result, we're about breaking even now on our out-of-pocket costs. It would seem that it pays to be nice to a commuter."

FRINGE AREA ANNEXATION [3]

Greater urbanization of the nation's people has been accompanied by greater suburbanization and the two-way process is

[3] From "Trends and Forecasts in Fringe Areas," article by John C. Bollens, associate professor, Department of Political Science, University of California at Los Angeles. *Public Management,* journal of the International City Managers' Association. 35:271-5. December 1953. Reprinted by permission.

continuing. Most of our population increase in the last decade has been in urban areas, but much of the gain within these areas has occurred in suburbs and fringes. A considerable part of the scattering of urban people over more land is taking place in territory adjacent to, but not legally part of, a municipality. The rate of population growth in some unincorporated fringe sectors is phenomenal. Numerous fringes have one fourth to one half as many residents as the neighboring city. A few are more populous than the nearby municipality itself. Over-all, several million urban residents in the United States now live in unincorporated urban areas.

Underlying most problems of fringe areas is one compelling fact: fringe residents are living in urban areas and yet they resist coming under the jurisdiction of comprehensive local governmental machinery capable of satisfying numerous community needs. In practice, they select a few public services that satisfy, sometimes only in part, their most acute needs. Most often they seek to acquire a few services from the county, the adjoining city, a special purpose district, or a private company. This piecemeal service arrangement may be fairly satisfactory when a fringe is first being occupied, but as growth mounts it becomes increasingly unrealistic. Nevertheless, many fringes are reluctant to meet the actual conditions facing them.

This reluctant, unrealistic approach causes most fringe areas to have several urban deficiencies and inferior conditions. Very prevalent is the lack of adequate planning guides and building regulations. Also frequent is poor or no drainage, sewers, or sanitation. Shortcomings in streets are often noticeable, including no streets, poor construction, substandard lighting, and no paving. Other significant weaknesses are in fire protection, water, law enforcement, health, recreation, smoke abatement, and transportation.

Such fringe conditions frequently have harmful effects within the entire urban area and become more serious as fringes become older. The casual observer may feel that if fringe residents want to live in this type of environment the decision should rest with them. This viewpoint, however, disregards an important consideration. The effects of fringe problem conditions are not con-

fined to the area causing them. Many times the shortcomings of
the fringe spill over and harass the neighboring municipality.
This is particularly apparent in health, law enforcement, and fire
protection activities. Thus, the growth of the fringe and its
weaknesses are usually matters of major importance and serious
consequences for cities. This is why the fringe-area problem is
one of the major questions currently confronting many municipal officials.

Because of recent widespread recognition that the problems
of the fringe quickly or ultimately become the problems of the
adjoining city, more and more municipalities are giving serious
attention to the matter. Although the largest part of the job lies
not behind but ahead, noteworthy study and action by some cities
give hope for a lessening of the fringe difficulty. Progress is
being made and patterns of problem solving are being worked
out and tested. Generally, however, the attainments have not so
far matched the seriousness and importance of the difficulty.
There is a real need for more cities both to study and act intelligently and comprehensively in the field of area adjustment.

Cities are using various approaches to the fringe-area problem. The most frequent method is annexation of adjacent urbanized territory. During a four-year period in the late 1930's, annexations were completed each year by an average of only forty-
eight cities. The number spurted as World War II came to a
conclusion and . . . [in 1953] 402 cities made annexations.
This is the highest total attained during the last fifteen years. . . .

Out of the extensive utilization of annexation has come
agreement that four elements are required for successful use of
this method of dealing with fringe problems. The first is that
annexation should be general and not selective. Spot annexations
of wealthy subdivisions or areas built up with streets and sewers
should not be the only guide for acquiring territory. Consideration must also be given to the long-term hazards of poorly developed fringe areas.

A second point of concurrence is that annexation should be
undertaken when the fringe is becoming urbanized and first
needing city services and before it is extensively developed. This

facilitates the use of proper controls when they will be most effective and avoids future economic waste.

The third requirement is that annexation should conform to sound financing and well-balanced, over-all development. Areas should be absorbed when a full complement of municipal services can be provided without long delay and within the financial ability of the city. Furthermore, intelligent development of the newly acquired area should not take place at the expense of the older parts of the city.

The fourth and final point of accord is that the city must accept leadership and responsibility in working out the problems of the city-fringe community so as to avoid curtailment of its own growth. Such leadership and responsibility require the obtaining of a comprehensive understanding of the fringe area coupled with the formulation of an intelligent program of information and action.

Although annexation is the most prevalent way of attacking the fringe-area problem, there are other methods which are lessening fringe difficulties with varying degrees of success. . . .

The first of these possibilities is limited annexation. Its objective is to provide necessary control and guidance in the development of new areas without taxation and without the obligation to furnish all city services to a scattered and lightly developed area. For example, voters in Austin, Texas, recently amended their charter to enable the city to annex fringe areas for limited zoning and sanitation purposes. In such areas the citizens may vote in councilmanic elections but not on bond issues. They do not pay city taxes and they receive no services except those for which they pay fees.

Another approach being utilized is the extraterritorial power of cities. All or certain classes of municipalities in some states have the right to exercise limited control over territory adjoining their borders. Such regulation usually consists of zoning, subdivision regulations and construction codes. Usually jurisdiction may be exercised over that part of the fringe which is within one or a few miles of the city boundaries. This can be a helpful device when available. However, it permits only a limited scope of control and frequently does not include the entire urban fringe.

A third type of method is the creation of special purpose districts. This type of local governmental unit is frequently used by fringe inhabitants who think they are going to have just a few public needs, but their demands expand as the area becomes more urbanized. If a city cannot induce a fringe to annex or lacks a sufficiently liberal annexation procedure, should its officials encourage the organization of special districts, each one of which is usually limited to performing a single function?

Generally city officials are unwilling to encourage formation of special districts. If they cannot discourage such a development, they are increasingly trying to see that two provisions are adopted: (1) the special district covers as large an area as can be justified, and (2) the directors of the special district are selected from among the officials of existing general local governmental units. It is felt that an area-wide district can better cope with its assignment, and a special district whose government board members are tied into existing general units is more likely to achieve much needed coordination.

A fourth option is incorporation [of the fringe area itself as an independent municipal unit] and the decision regarding its use is a matter of initiation and judgment by the voting residents of the urban fringe. More often it is being realized that incorporation is not always an intelligent answer. Many fringe areas have insufficient taxable resources to support the range of services desired by their inhabitants, a situation that is almost always present if the area is largely residential.

When incorporation is contemplated, the high cost of certain types of sewers, water lines and other installations is frequently overlooked. Under such circumstances a fringe which is substandard may through incorporation simply become a low quality municipality. In addition, this new city may be highly uncooperative toward the municipality which it continues to border. Some cities, including Cincinnati and Wichita, emphatically oppose fringe incorporations.

Encouraging the county to act in certain fields of control where it already has power to exercise authority can sometimes be used as an approach to reducing fringe difficulties, At times such activity by the county requires added legal authorization. Very often, however, counties, either due to individual choice or legal inability, are not active in exercising regulations in sanitation, health, zoning and subdividing.

Related to this increased role of the county is legislation which has very recently gone into effect in California. Under it the county supervisors may on their own initiative or on petition of the voters establish a county-administered service area in which services above the general county standard can be furnished and for which additional taxes are levied.

The sale of city services to the fringe is a final method to be mentioned here and one about which there is considerable controversy. A growing number of cities are refusing to respond to the fringe's request for one or more functions. Without good cost records and adequate contractual safeguards the city may find itself performing services for the fringe area at the expense of its own taxpayers. Futhermore, this practice delays the annexation process, and fringe dwellers who receive selected services through the city have no incentive to become part of the city. This effect is counterbalanced to some extent by charging outside consumers at rates considerably higher than those paid by city residents.

Except for extraordinary situations such as the immediate prevention of hazardous or seriously harmful conditions, the trend is for cities not to respond to fringe requests for one or more services. Response by a city nourishes the continuance of the fringe and works directly counter to efforts of the city to solve the deficiencies permanently. Such assistance often makes living in the fringe financially advantageous.

Trends in fringe areas indicate that no one best solution can be applied to the fringe problem for all urban areas or even for cities within a single state. For most situations annexation is the best answer that has been devised up to this time. Many larger cities, however, are practically or entirely surrounded by incorporated places. Action on their need, which frequently has not progressed further than discussion, extends beyond fringe considerations and calls for some type of true metropolitan government.

An important factor contributing to the effectiveness of other methods of eliminating or reducing fringe areas is the need for cities to make themselves more attractive places in which to live. Making cities more livable communities can be an effective and often decisive counterbalance to the real or imagined attractions of fringes.

Abolition of excessive noise, dirt, and nuisances, modernization of building, housing, fire, and zoning codes, rehabilitation of blighted areas, formulation of well-founded subdivision regulations, and provision of desired services with the highest possible efficiency and imaginativeness—some or all of these are challenges confronting the officials and citizens of most cities of the United States.

A REGIONAL MASTER PLAN [4]

It is a challenge to the civic, commercial, industrial, and governmental leaders in . . . [an area of closely linked communities] to adopt and carry out a program of development and control on a regional basis to embody those over-all functions and activities which are common to all of the individual jurisdictions, but which individually they are physically, financially and technically unable to effectuate.

Such over-all regional control need not interfere with or duplicate normal administration and services at the local levels, but would rather consolidate the major functions and problems confronting them for their common solution and benefit. Such functions could conceivably include: Regional planning and zoning; sanitary drainage and flood control; major thoroughfares and transportation; water supply; uniform building regulations; regional school systems; and others.

Any such scheme of administrative control over the future development of our metropolitan centers must be sufficiently comprehensive and all-inclusive of the numerous factors involved

⁴ From "Controlling Regional Development," article by Joseph F. Base, city manager, Santa Clara, California. *Public Works.* 85:134-5. March 1954. Reprinted by permission.

in order that such control will contribute materially to the best interests of the whole region. Recognition of only the local phases of the problem cannot aid in properly shaping the growth of the whole in conformance with modern thought as to what shall constitute the ideal metropolitan community of the future. The ground-work must be laid upon a broad and firm basis.

We cannot continue to build and govern our communities without a comprehensive plan, an over-all specification and definite long range schedule. In projecting such a plan it is imperative that considerable thought be given to the condition of the undeveloped areas of the community well in advance of their subdivision into residential, commercial or industrial districts. This necessitates a study of the legal as well as physical aspects of the areas lying within the limits of a region so extensive as to be inclusive of all the territory and population which may probably ever become a part of the metropolitan community.

Legal aspects which should be considered involve primarily the following: (1) Recognition of the regional character of the problem. (2) Provisions for the permanent organization of the regional areas into a governmental subdivision having adequate powers to control the development within its boundaries. (3) Adequate consideration of the rural as well as the urban populations so that the interests of both may be respected and safe-guarded. (4) Preparation and enforcement of regulations to govern all developments within the regional areas with the object of consolidating such developments into a comprehensive regional scheme.

Physical aspects involved should necessarily include a study of: (1) The entire area to be included in the regional organization, the boundaries of which are projected into the future as far as can be consistently estimated, preferably to the limits of the requirements of the ultimate maximum population. (2) A physical study of the area involved including topography for economic development; agricultural possibilities; underground deposits of commercial value; and preparation of a regional master plan giving recognition to the foregoing.

(3) A comprehensive long range plan of major improvements and utilities extensions covering the entire regional area

and conforming to the master plan, as for example, comprehensive sewerage systems, involving trunk and outfall lines, together with necessary treatment works, and water supply and transmission systems. (4) Provision for various public projects such as forest preserves and park areas; recreation; building restrictions; land uses; and area and population density restrictions. (5) Provisions for uniform building control to cover type of buildings, their construction and the regulation of architectural treatment so far as legally possible.

It is believed that the scope of this problem is so extensive and concerns the people at large to such a degree that it should come within the powers of the state. Enabling legislation should be provided which will create a regional planning authority to include all the territory which may ultimately be one community. The boundaries of such a district should be carefully determined, accurately and legally described, platted and recorded. No exception should be made of any incorporated places or other areas. The entire district should be created and treated as a whole.

Provisions for the financial maintenance of such an organization could be made by appropriating a portion of local or state taxes for this purpose; or the necessary moneys could be raised in a manner similar to that adopted in specially created districts organized for sanitary, public health, and other purposes. The intention would be to consolidate a number of separate activities now performed by many individual local jurisdictions, rather than to superimpose yet another new governmental monstrosity on the already tottering heap.

(1) Create a representative regional group of business and professional people, also public officials and administrators from local, county and state levels. (2) Establish a fund to defray research, technical, and related expenses. (3) Obtain suitable quarters, preferably without cost, for use of regional group and staff. (4) Organize the regional commission. (5) Recruit the research and technical staff. (6) Prepare and adopt a work program to include: (a) Delineation of the ultimate boundaries of the proposed regional area; (b) Establishment of geographical districts or zones to facilitate study and ultimate administration. (c) Exploration of legislation and frameworks of other regional

organizations. (d) Study of needed legislation. (e) Cooperation of state legislators. (f) Public education.

In summary, my suggestion is to establish a regional master plan, legalize its boundaries, and activate an organization with powers and authority to insure the orderly development and administration of the . . . [regional area] as an aid to solving present difficulties and to make a contribution to better living for the generations to come.

VI. FEDERAL AND STATE ROLES IN PLANNING

EDITOR'S INTRODUCTION

Community planning is commonly considered a local function, and so it is, for the most part. Yet the Federal Government and the states play important roles in community planning activities. This is true principally because of the funds and technical advice available from the Federal Government, and because the states, under our form of government, retain the right to withhold or grant powers to their communities in every phase of their activities.

This section reviews the most recent and most far-reaching Federal legislation affecting community planning—the Housing Act of 1949 and the Housing Act of 1954, under which the so-called "workable program" theory has developed. This is followed by a discussion of a proposed Federal Department of "Urbiculture," devoted solely to urban problems.

In 1953 President Eisenhower proposed and Congress approved the creation of a Commission on Intergovernmental Relations, to study the proper relationships among Federal, state and local governments in the framework of today's conditions. The commission completed its report in 1955, and its recommendations pertaining to planning and directly related subjects are included in this section.

The limitations frequently imposed upon communities by their state governments are described by Senator Desmond. The final article in this section discusses the planner's place in politics, at all the various levels mentioned above.

FEDERAL ROLE IN REDEVELOPMENT [1]

The crisis of American cities has been viewed with alarm for decades. The decay and obsolescence of the central sections of

[1] From "Rebuilding American Cities—the Challenge of Urban Redevelopment," article by Nathaniel S. Keith, redevelopment consultant and former director, Federal Urban Redevelopment Program. *American Scholar.* 23:341-52. Summer 1954. Reprinted by permission.

our metropolitan areas, the spread of slums and blight, the quickening tempo of the flight to the suburbs have been of increasing concern to municipal officials, city planners, newspaper editors, union officials, downtown merchants, and certain segments of the real estate and banking fraternity. This is to mention only a few of the groups which react strongly to the state of affairs in our cities as places in which to live, work and capitalize on investments.

Over the past ten to fifteen years, the growing attention to the plight of American cities has given rise to countless discussions, to numerous investigations and political inquiries, and to many proposed panaceas. Some of the latter have been on a very rarefied plane, proposing a complete recasting of the physical structure of cities on a scale comparable to rebuilding after an atomic bombardment. Others, at the opposite extreme, have grossly oversimplified the problem as merely a matter of requiring the owners of substandard properties to make minimum repairs. . . .

Between these extremes, however, there has developed increasing recognition that the hard core of the crisis of American cities lies in the physical obsolescence of much of their central sections and that feasible solutions to that crisis must involve ways and means of removing those obsolete physical structures. In short, this is the principle of urban redevelopment.

This is not to say that there are not many other equally crucial symptoms of the ills of our cities: over-all congestion, distorted land uses, traffic jams, inadequate parking, horse-and-buggy street patterns, insufficient or obsolete community facilities, smoke and smog, and river pollution. It certainly is not to deny that the plight of our cities reflects the absence of planning when they were first developed and that efforts to remedy that plight make sense only within a framework of up-to-date and realistic city planning.

But it is definitely to say that a comprehensive attack on those ills can progress only if the way is cleared of the brick and mortar of worn-out and misplaced structures, which in the main represent private property and are usually too expensive for private enterprise to acquire merely for purposes of demolition.

. . . [In 1949] Congress took a far-reaching step to help solve this problem. This was done under Title I of the Housing Act of 1949 by authorizing Federal loans of $1 billion and capital grants of $500 million to assist cities in carrying out urban redevelopment projects. The theory was that by the combination of Federal financial assistance and the use of local powers of eminent domain, it should be possible to assemble sizable blocks of the blighted real estate that lies athwart the rebuilding of central sections of cities, to clear that land and write down its cost to a feasible value for new development, and to sell or lease it primarily to private enterprise for rebuilding in accordance with a definite local plan of land use. The law further required that the redevelopment plan for each project be in accord with a general plan for the development of the locality as a whole.

This program, new and untested and without substantial precedent, has been slow in gathering momentum. But by . . . [1954] approximately sixty projects . . . [were] under way in over thirty cities. These involve the acquisition and clearance of over two thousand acres of slums and blighted areas. Their re-development—in new housing, public improvements, or new commercial or industrial facilities—will involve an investment of about $600 million, primarily in private funds. In about seventy other communities, projects involving over three thousand acres of blighted city land are in the final stages of planning, while about 120 other localities are in the process of selecting their first project areas. In short, all cities with population of over one million, most of the middle-sized cities and many of the smaller ones have redevelopment programs under way or on the planning boards. . . .

Behind this varied and growing support for redevelopment lie the shocking dimensions of slums and blighted areas in this country. The statistics show that in 1950, over 11.5 million dwelling units or 30 per cent of the non-farm housing supply were delapidated, or lacking private indoor flush toilet or bath or hot or cold running water. While a considerable proportion of these dwellings could be subject to repairs or the installation of standard sanitary facilities, there is general agreement that from 5 million to 7 million units are beyond hope of salvage and are ripe only for demolition.

While there is considerable variation among cities in the ratio of poor housing to good housing, the slum problem is a universal one among American communities, with the possible exception of a few of the most exclusive bedroom suburbs of large metropolitan areas. During the four years that I headed the Federal urban redevelopment program, I personally inspected the slums of more than sixty cities from east to west and from north to south and gained a paper knowledge of the slums of another two-hundred-odd communities. There are the tenements of Boston and New York, which were ready-made but durable slums from their inception. There are the mansions-converted-into-slums of Cleveland, Chicago and Los Angeles. There are the miserable . . . shanties of the South and the "skid rows" and Mexican "shack towns" of the West. In fact, in my travels I encountered a curious spirit of competition among local officials who would frequently boast to me that their community has "the worst . . . slums in the country."

However, the problems created by blight and obsolescence cut wider than the shameful living conditions of the slums. The slums are heavy deficit areas from the standpoint of city treasuries. Many of them are in locations now totally unsuited for residential use but which could provide much needed room for expansion and modernization of downtown business and commerce. Many of them freeze hopelessly outdated street patterns and frustrate the quest for open space and ease of circulation, which are among the primary facts of life in the fight against urban congestion. In short, our cities are struggling with an obsolete physical pattern which developed without anticipation of the tremendous expansion of urban population within the past half-century or of the revolution in living habits caused by the gasoline engine.

An equally potent factor in the support for urban redevelopment is the need for public underwriting of its cost. At least nine times out of ten, it will cost substantially more to acquire built-up city real estate—even though it be severely blighted—than can be recovered from selling the underlying land at a price that will be attractive and feasible for new private development. . . .

Furthermore, given the existing allocation of the tax dollar between the Federal and local governments and the costs of essential municipal services, the Federal treasury must absorb the bulk of the cost of urban redevelopment. Redevelopment laws were on the statute books of twenty-four of the most populous states prior to the passage of the [1949] Federal law; with few exceptions there had been no activity under them due primarily to the lack of state or local financing. . . .

The justification for spending Federal funds for redevelopment is a matter of the national benefits attached to maintaining the vitality of American cities. From a strictly dollars-and-cents standpoint, which is only one of the many considerations, the experience to date indicates that every Federal dollar spent for capital grants will make possible about six to seven dollars in new private and public investment in the rebuilding of blighted areas. More important than this, in my opinion, are the benefits from combating urban decay. Since the economic strength of the nation rests primarily in its cities, it should follow that measures to keep cities physically equipped for modern living are at least as essential as Federal aid for soil reclamation, crop price support or shipbuilding.

A further strong influence in support of redevelopment over the next year will be the example of the guinea-pig projects now under way. There is no need to claim perfection for these projects in all their details. The important fact is that they are proving that urban redevelopment will work. They are generally reducing the density of population in congested areas, drastically cutting the percentage of land covered by buildings, and developing new street systems, frequently in conjunction with other major traffic improvements. They are clearing slums which for decades have withstood the well-meaning efforts of civic organizations lacking the ammunition for effective attacks upon them. They are attracting private capital into the rebuilding of central sections of cities where private capital was unable or unwilling to venture before. . . .

Philadelphia is . . . in the process of a major face-lifting operation through redevelopment, which was begun under the old Republican regime and is being pressed by the new Democratic regime of Mayor Clark. Redevelopment projects are under way or projected in three blighted urban neighborhoods which will lead to about 2,800 new dwelling units, with schools, playgrounds and new shopping area. Also well advanced are plans for a new city within a city in the Eastwick section, a swampy area of some four square miles in the southeastern corner of the city. Now a hodge-podge of scattered shack towns, this area, after clearing and filling, is projected as a new community of 15,000 houses and apartments, complete with schools, parks and shopping centers, and including a new industrial district of about nine hundred acres. . . .

During the many years that Congress has intermittently examined the nation's slum problem, a favorite newspaper device for illustrating stories on these investigations has been a photograph of sordid alley shacks in Washington, D.C., with the dome of the Capitol rising majestically in the background. Many of these shacks still stand; others have been removed in piecemeal fashion. Finally, the surgical approach is being used on a seventy-seven-acre tract in southwest Washington, now a heavily built-up slum area bordering the Washington waterfront and within easy access of the business section and Capitol Hill. Here nine hundred units of new housing will be developed, along with expanded recreational facilities, new stores, and the right-of-way for a major new expressway which will cross one corner of the project. This is only the first bite in a longer-range program for the full redevelopment of southwest Washington.

In the Midwest, Chicago is redeveloping 101 acres of congested slums on the Southside under a plan calling for 2,000 apartments, largely in high-rise buildings commanding a near view of Lake Michigan, for a major shopping center and for a park and school site, with only about 10 per cent of the land to be covered by buildings. In a second project, located just one mile from the Loop in an area surrounded by industrial and commercial development, a fifty-acre pocket of ancient slums is being cleared for redevelopment as a planned light industrial district. These are the forerunners of an extensive program which will also tackle the problem of reclaiming thousands of acres of vacant land in "dead" subdivisions on the outskirts of the city, derelicts of the speculative real estate boom of the twenties.

One of the most dramatic demonstrations of redevelopment is the "Capitol Approach" program in St. Paul. Here, the Minnesota capitol is being rescued from the blighted environment of 190 acres of run-down houses and a patchwork of obsolete streets. The immediate approach to the capitol, involving about one third of the acreage, has been acquired through state and city funds and is being laid out in an open plan of parkways, malls, and sites for new public buildings. Flanking the capitol to the east and west, two redevelopment projects involving over 120 acres are under way. The old street pattern will be abandoned for a new design of parkways to carry through traffic and to serve as buffers for the rebuilt areas. About 1,250 apartments will be built, together with neighborhood parks, schools, and private office buildings and stores. . . .

These [examples] are encouraging beginnings, offering good evidence of the feasibility of redevelopment but only scratching the surface of the total problem. . . .

The relatively slow pace of redevelopment thus far is understandable in terms of the complexity and novelty of the undertaking. While redevelopment can never become a simple or automatic process, there is ample evidence that with this experience behind them, the local redevelopment agencies can move ahead with their second and third run of projects much more rapidly.

The support for redevelopment is reaching into quarters which should prove effective in quieting local opposition, such as that stemming from slum landlordism, and also prove helpful in advancing the program on the national plane. In most cities, the downtown banks, the large downtown merchants and the other business establishments with a stake in the revival of central business districts are supporters of redevelopment. Builders, real estate investors and mortgage-lending institutions are showing greater interest in a program which is beginning to offer opportunities for large-scale construction in central locations.

Joined with these sources of support are most city governments, civic-minded organizations and organized labor.

As to the status of redevelopment in the Washington scene today, the situation is more complex. On the one hand, . . . [Congress has enacted] legislation embracing the recommendations of the President's advisory committee for a broadened program. [See "Urban Renewal Under the Housing Act of 1954" in this section below.] On the other hand, the execution of such a program must cope with the pressure for public retrenchment and run the gantlet of those groups in Congress and elsewhere which view most Federal grant-in-aid programs with skepticism if not with suspicion. Furthermore, it will face the flirtation of some influential groups with rehabilitation and various "fix-up" plans as a cheap substitute for the basic job of rebuilding. . . .

Whether sufficient push will emerge to carry redevelopment to full maturity in the near future is a much more uncertain question. A case in point is that the Administration has not backed up its support with a request for increased program funds at this time. Nevertheless, in my opinion, now is the time to press for continuity in redevelopment on a much broader scale. I believe a realistic objective would be a program of $2 billion additional in Federal grants, contemplating eventual expenditure of these funds at an average rate of about $250 million a year. This would represent a little more than one third of 1 per cent of the present Federal budget and perhaps one half of 1 per cent of the minimum achievable Federal budget.

On such a scale, redevelopment would have the opportunity to progress to maturity. A program of this size would clear 40,000 to 50,000 acres in the most congested areas, removing perhaps a million substandard dwellings. It would open up those areas for rebuilding on modern plans providing for ease of circulation and substantial open space. It would stimulate directly a new investment of $12 billion to $14 billion in housing, commercial and industrial facilities and public improvements. It would indirectly stimulate substantial additional off-site expenditures for rehousing and public improvements.

I do not pretend that such a program would bring on the millennium in urban life. But it would provide a solid base for the revitalization of the central sections of cities and for reversing the long-term trend of urban decay. In view of the mounting pressures for relief of the crisis of our cities and the impact of that crisis on our huge concentration of urban population, this may well prove to be an achievable objective within the not too distant future.

URBAN RENEWAL UNDER THE HOUSING ACT OF 1954 [2]

Urban renewal is the Eisenhower Administration's new term for the prevention and elimination of urban decay—slums and blight. To slum clearance and urban redevelopment under the Housing Act of 1949, urban renewal adds the concept of conservation and rehabilitation in treating these decaying and decayed areas [See "Federal Role in Redevelopment" in this section, above.] It is a more inclusive term than urban redevelopment and offers cities a real opportunity to make major inroads upon their blighted areas. The amount of financial assistance is considerable; [and] technical assistance is available for the asking. . . .

The urban renewal program can be broken down into three major areas—self help, financial assistance for public agencies, and assistance in private financing. The first—self help—requires each city that wishes to participate in the program to demonstrate that it has, or will have, a workable program to eliminate and prevent slums and blight. The second—financial assistance to public agencies—provides Federal financial assistance for two thirds of the cost of clearing a slum area or conserving a deteriorating area that is not yet slum but on its way. The third—assistance in private financing—provides special mortgage insurance under FHA to assist owners and builders in renovating and constructing housing in these redevelopment or conservation areas. All three form a package; each is a necessary part of the whole but each part can be discussed separately.

[2] From "Urban Renewal—a Program for Cities," article by William L. Slayton, assistant director, National Association of Housing and Redevelopment Officials. *Public Management*, journal of the International City Managers' Association. 37:74-7. April 1955. Reprinted by permission.

In adopting the Housing Act of 1954, Congress took the position that Federal financial assistance should not be granted those cities that did not face up to the problems of slums and blight. Before the Federal Government will enter into contracts for financial assistance for urban renewal projects, the locality must demonstrate that it has a "workable program" or that it is at least on the way to achieving a workable program for the elimination of slums and blight. In substance this means that the city must have done or must plan to do several things. The Housing and Home Finance Agency lists seven elements under this workable program, and the city interested in obtaining financial aid for urban renewal must make a formal submission on what it has done or plans to do in respect to each of these elements. These elements are:

1. Codes and ordinances. The locality must demonstrate that it has, or will have, adequate codes and ordinances covering minimum housing standards for existing and new dwellings.

2. A general plan for the community.

3. Identification of the areas of bad housing conditions and a plan of action to remedy such conditions.

4. An administrative organization for enforcing the codes and ordinances under Item 1.

5. Provision for the additional funds necessary to handle increased activity in enforcement, planning, and so on.

6. A recognition of the problem of rehousing families displaced because of urban renewal activities.

7. Evidence of community understanding of, and participation in, the urban renewal program.

The Housing and Home Finance Agency will review this material, and if it finds it adequate HHFA will certify that the locality meets the workable program requirement. This certification is good for one year. If a city wishes to obtain financial assistance for additional projects after the year has elapsed, the workable program must be recertified.

Approval of the workable program, however, does not automatically entitle the city to a check from HHFA. Having an approved workable program merely makes it possible for HHFA

to grant financial assistance for specific projects. Other requirements must be met for specific urban renewal projects.

An urban renewal project is much like a slum clearance and
urban redevelopment project under the Housing Act of 1949 except that it may cover a broader range of activities than could
the redevelopment project. The financing is much the same: the
Federal Government agrees to pay two thirds of the net cost of
the undertaking and the locality must put up one third. This
one third, however, does not have to be in direct appropriations
but can be in the form of public improvements—streets, schools,
playgrounds, and so on. The advantage of the Housing Act of
1954 is that this broadened activity permits the locality to treat
larger areas and provide more varied treatment than just clearance and rebuilding.

Just what can a city do under the urban renewal provisions
of the Housing Act of 1954? It can of course clear a slum area,
install the necessary site improvements, and sell or lease the land
to private developers for development in accordance with the
redevelopment plan for the area. The difference between the
costs (the sum of the cost of the land, the demolition of the
structures, and the administrative costs) and the resale value of
the land constitutes the net cost of the project. The Federal
Government agrees to pay two thirds of this cost. The locality
puts up the remaining one third, its public improvements count-
ing as credit against its one-third share. This is the typical redevelopment project under the Housing Act of 1949.

But under the housing act of 1954 the locality can obtain
Federal aid even when it does not demolish the houses. It must,
however, undertake activity in an area that results in substantial
improvement of the houses and environment. It does not have
to acquire the property and resell it. Although on the face of it
this procedure may seem a good deal simpler than the redevelopment process, it presents a good many problems some of which
require additional state legislation before they can be met.

These nonredevelopment-type urban renewal projects (conservation and rehabilitation) work out something like this. The
city delineates an area where it feels housing conditions are such
that the structures do not need to be torn down but can be fixed

up to make them acceptable living quarters. It then prepares a plan for the area. Such a plan should provide for (1) the demolition of those structures that are beyond rehabilitation; (2) the installation of public improvements that are needed to improve the area (playgrounds, parks, street lights, new street surfacing), (3) the redesign of the land use pattern wherever possible (closing streets, widening streets); (4) removal of adverse and/or nonconforming uses; and (5) a program for encouraging voluntary rehabilitation by the owners of those structures worth rehabilitating.

The Federal Government agrees to foot two thirds of the cost of such a project. The cost includes the preparation of the plan, the cost of the public improvements, the net cost of any property that has to be acquired, and the cost of carrying out the voluntary rehabilitation program. The basic theory behind this approach is that the decline of these areas is due in part to the inadequacy (both in quality and quantity) of the public improvements.

In addition, the basic land use pattern of the area may be such that it creates deteriorating factors. A replanning operation, closing off streets to change the traffic pattern, for example, may be sufficient to remove a basic cause of the area's deteriorating. By installing the public improvements and by creating a basically sound, or at least a considerably improved, land use pattern, the property owners in the area are given cause to invest money in their property. With this as a base the city can undertake a voluntary rehabilitation program among the owners.

All of this is easy to say, harder to do. Cities have had little experience with this kind of program; much is yet to be learned. But the incentive is considerable. The Federal Government feels that this approach offers a great deal and is willing to back up its faith by paying two thirds of the bill. This means that the Federal Government will pay for two thirds of the cost of public improvements installed in the area so long as they are designed to serve the area and are part of the renewal plan for the area.

The city must also demonstrate that it has a program that will result in the substantial improvement of housing conditions in the area. HHFA is not writing any blank checks; it will require quite a documentation of the proposed plans and will have to approve what the city plans to do before it will advance any money for the project. Its requirements are not simple—sometimes they seem quite picayune. But certainly they are aimed at making sure that the city makes proper use of the funds advanced by the Federal Government. . . .

The result is the renewal of the area—improved public facilities, improved land use pattern, improved housing conditions. It is a major opportunity for cities to obtain substantial assistance to help themselves.

Private financing might not seem to have much interest to public officials, but in the urban renewal program it becomes an extremely important element. This business of voluntary rehabilitation is not simple. People without funds cannot very well spend substantial funds in improving their homes. If financing were available for substantial home improvements, voluntary rehabilitation would be given a considerable boost.

This is precisely what was done in the Housing Act of 1954. One of the problems in improving existing housing in these areas is that of obtaining loans. FHA and lending institutions have taken the position that the condition of these areas did not warrant loans on individual structures regardless of the condition of the structure itself. They reasoned that the character of the area held down the value of the property regardless of the quality of the structure.

The Housing Act of 1954 provided for a special financing vehicle to remedy this situation. Section 220 was designed to be used in urban renewal areas and in such areas only. A special insurance fund was set up for this section, and Congress specifically told FHA not to use its standard "economic soundness test" in evaluating properties for 220 mortgage insurance. FHA is supposed to take into consideration what the city proposes to do, what the renewal plan for the area calls for, and to base its valuations on these criteria rather than on existing conditions.

This approach is of tremendous significance. It means that a house in the area will be eligible for substantial loans for major rehabilitation work, whereas under previous legislation and valuation practice it would not be. It gives recognition to the plans of the city itself, but at the same time of course places consider-able responsibility upon the city to be sure to live up to its re-newal plans. With this kind of mortgage insurance available, lending institutions will be willing to advance the kind of money necessary to make rehabilitation possible. Without this kind of financing assistance, a program of voluntary rehabilitation is al-most bound to fail.

These then are the three new elements of the urban renewal program—the city's workable program, the city's urban renewal project, and mortgage insurance for the rehabilitation of struc-tures. They are in addition to the slum clearance and urban re-development program that is a part of urban renewal. With the Federal Government now offering substantial financial assistance for rehabilitation and conservation projects, as well as for slum clearance and urban redevelopment projects, cities have never been in such a good position to take really effective action against their blighted and slum areas.

DEPARTMENT OF URBICULTURE [3]

Urbiculture, as I conceive it, is what you might call an art, or a science of developing and cultivating urban land to its best and highest use.

The fact that there is a Federal need for a department of this kind is so clear to me that, personally, I am always inclined to oversimplify the reasons but, fundamentally, it follows very much the argument that was advanced for the establishment of the Department of Agriculture.

In 1862, when the Department of Agriculture was estab-lished, approximately 80 per cent of our population lived on farms or in rural areas, and only 20 per cent in urban territory. Now, . . . that situation has entirely changed, and we now find that roughly 85 per cent of our total population lives in urban territory and only 15 per cent in what might be termed rural or farm areas.

[3] From statement by Representative J. Arthur Younger (Republican, California). In *Creation of a Department of Urbiculture*; hearing, July 26, 1955, before a sub-committee of the House Committee on Government Operations. 84th Congress, 1st session. The Committee. Washington 25, D.C. 1955. p3-4.

The tremendous job which the Department of Agriculture has done is best illustrated by the fact that when it was created, it took approximately 80 per cent of our population to produce the food and fiber for themselves and for the balance of the population, while now 15 per cent of the population produces the food and fiber for our entire population, and in addition we have a tremendous surplus with which the Government is wrestling all the time.

Naturally, the problems of our people arise from the concentration of population. In 1862 the problems which came to the Federal Government for solution arose from the rural areas because 80 per cent of the population lived in the rural areas.

With 85 per cent of the population concentrated in the urban areas, naturally the problems which come to the Federal Government for solution arise from those areas, and the Federal Government has recognized these problems because it has dealt with them continuously, and in a continuing wider field all the time, by Federal legislation, as, for instance, on the questions of health, housing, crime, smog control, civil defense, and so forth. All of those problems come to the Federal Government. . . .

We have now independent agencies in the Federal Government that deal solely with municipalities which should be concentrated in the one area. For instance, we have the District of Columbia; we have the District of Columbia Redevelopment Land Agency, we have the National Capital Housing Authority; the National Capital Planning Agency; the Housing and Home Finance Agency, and the Federal Civil Defense Administration as well as the Small Business Administration. Those are just a few of the independent agencies which deal almost exclusively with population and with problems that arise in and out of the city population.

There are branches and segments of a number of other departments that would naturally fall into a new department were a department created, such as smog control, certain phases of educational programs and juvenile delinquency. We are increasing our attention to that problem right along. . . .

The Federal Government has already done quite a bit of work in the field of juvenile delinquency through studies and investigations. For instance, there is a committee in the Senate which has been investigating juvenile delinquency. You also have the problem of narcotics, which is a Federal problem and, primarily, the problems that arise out of the traffic in narcotics is a city problem. You have very little difficulty in the rural or farm areas with narcotics. It is practically all concentrated in the cities.

It has been my observation . . . that these independent agencies, by and large, do not do as good a job as the departments which have a head sitting at Cabinet level. While these independent agencies theoretically deal direct with the Executive head of the Government, is not so easy for them to deal that way as it is for a Cabinet officer. I think that as long as we are in this field that we should concentrate these various Federal projects, Federal agencies, Federal grants and Federal concern over the problems that originate in the city areas into a department that does have a head with a Cabinet status.

In simple terms, that is what . . . [the bill to create a Department of Urbiculture (H.R. 1864) is] designed to do.

ASSESSING GOVERNMENTAL RESPONSIBILITIES [4]

The Commission [on Intergovernmental Relations] has noted the magnitude of the housing problem which confronts the nation today. The latest census revealed that despite the efforts of private initiative, municipalities, the national government, and some states, there were 15 million substandard homes, of which 10 million were located in urban centers. The growth of slums in the centers of cities produces a vicious circle for municipal governments. Increased poverty, crime, and juvenile delinquency necessitate increased municipal expenditures for police protection, public assistance, and other social services. At the same time, slum area properties yield less and less municipal revenue; this in turn, requires the levy of additional taxes on other properties. . . .

The Commission believes that responsibility for the initiation and administration of public housing, slum clearance, and urban renewal programs rests with state and local governments. States should supply guidance, and localities should take positive action

[4] From *Report to the President for Transmittal to the Congress*. United States. Commission on Intergovernmental Relations. Superintendent of Documents. Washington 25, D.C. 1955. p225-32.

(1) to develop over-all city and metropolitan area plans, (2) to adopt and administer vigorously local housing codes, building codes, and zoning, subdivision, and planning regulations, and (3) to coordinate and execute neighborhood conservation plans.

The shocking neglect of many municipal governments in failing to enforce and modernize existing housing and building codes has done much to bring about widespread conditions of urban blight and has resulted in governmental subsidies on an increasing scale. Local governments should accept responsibility for the broad goals of raising housing standards, eliminating and preventing slums and blight, establishing and preserving sound neighborhoods, and laying a foundation for healthy community development. Local governments should recognize the interrelationship of these activities and should work continuously to improve administrative and fiscal coordination among all local agencies and programs involved in planning, development and enforcement of codes and ordinances, slum clearance, public housing, and other related elements.

The commission recommends that state governments assume considerably increased responsibility for meeting housing needs which are beyond the combined resources of private initiative and local units of government. Specifically, the commission recommends that:

(a) States lend financial, technical, and professional assistance to localities on the basis of need;

(b) States provide enabling legislation to encourage their subdivisions to adopt by reference modern and uniform building, housing, and sanitary codes;

(c) States provide for the establishment of metropolitan planning agencies to assist in redefining city limits and in providing for the integrated design of new suburban areas;

(d) States assume responsibility for working out appropriate, interstate compacts or agreements in the event of jurisdictional problems among them with assistance and leadership from the national government when required.

The commission believes that a positive program at the state level would reduce municipal demands upon the national government. The commission believes that many states have failed to meet their responsibilities in the field of housing. Federal aid for low-rent housing and slum clearance originated because of the inability or unwillingness of the municipalities, but more generally, the unwillingness of states, to meet and solve their problems. Fortunately, there have been exceptions. A few states have taken vigorous action to meet the housing and slum clearance needs of their municipalities.

The commission believes that regulatory activities and the exercise of the police power with respect to housing conditions belong solely with the states and localities. But it is both appropriate and desirable for the national government to encourage more state and local action by making such action a condition of Federal grants for slum clearance and urban renewal. These interconnected actions must be taken to avoid a situation whereby the national government finances slum clearance and urban renewal projects in one area of a city, while the municipal government allows other areas to deteriorate to the point where still more Federal aid is requested.

The commission recommends that the national government continue, with certain modifications noted below, technical and financial assistance to state and local governments for slum clearance and urban renewal, metropolitan area planning, and low-rent public housing.

The commission is convinced that action of the most vigorous sort must be undertaken by both private and public agencies to combat slum conditions and urban blight, which are creating increasingly serious financial and social problems for many of the larger municipalities and densely populated states. The commission believes it entirely appropriate and essential for the national government to exercise strong leadership in this endeavor, not only in consideration of the general national welfare but also in terms of furthering civil defense preparedness in the United States.

Without reference to the merits of public, as contrasted to privately constructed, housing for low-income groups, the commission believes that to the extent that government, at whatever level, continues to provide or subsidize low-rent housing, it is appropriate for the national government to furnish leadership, stimulation, and technical and financial assistance when needed by the state and local governments.

The commission submits several specific recommendations and suggestions for changes in current programs of housing and urban renewal which it believes will improve the effectiveness of those programs and will facilitate national-state-local relationships in this field.

The commission recommends that Congress provide that national technical and financial assistance be administered on a state basis where the state establishes by law comprehensive programs of public housing and slum clearance including significant state financial aid.

In some of the preceding recommendations the commission has urged considerably increased state action on municipal problems of housing and slum clearance. The commission believes that the present pattern of direct national-local relationships is clearly justified where states have failed to take positive action in the field of housing and urban renewal. The national government, however, has deliberately sought direct relationships with local governments in the field of housing and has not endeavored to get relationships onto a state basis in the few cases where states have taken positive action (for example, New York and Pennsylvania). In these instances, state-local and national-local programs have operated side by side within a given state, resulting no doubt in less than full utilization of combined national-state-local initiative and resources. The situation in New York State is a clear example. Furthermore, particularly with respect to public housing, there has been little financial inducement to state activity, because the national government carries most of the burden. Increased state action can hardly be expected unless the national government consents to take into full partnership those states willing to assume increased responsibilities.

The commission recommends that states and municipalities give increased attention to unifying their community services through the creation of metropolitan planning authorities to deal with problems related to urban affairs. The commission further recommends that the states provide enabling legislation as well as financial assistance and professional and technical consultation and guidance where the locality is not able to meet its own planning needs. The national government should provide leadership through research on community design and layout and the dissemination of information on methods for achieving improvement in local planning. The provisions of current legislation providing Federal fifty-fifty matching grants to states and municipalities for metropolitan area planning should be continued. . . .

The problems peculiar to metropolitan areas call for increased attention and action by all levels of government. These problems, as typified by centers of urban blight in the wake of migration to the suburbs, are particularly acute in the fields of housing and urban renewal. Promotion of metropolitan area planning by the national government is both appropriate and desirable. Local initiative and responsibility should be relied upon to a maximum, and should be supplemented by state planning efforts, and by technical assistance from the national government in cases where combined community and state resources are inadequate to meet the need.

The commission recommends that in planning future slum clearance and public housing projects, all levels of government give serious attention to the problem of urban decentralization for defense.

The need for decentralization of congested urban centers in the interest of reduced vulnerability to nuclear weapon attack is self-evident. In each decade, normal construction volume provides homes for 30 million people, as well as the supporting shops, roads, and factories necessary to serve and supply them. At this rate, 60 million people are "relocated" over a twenty-year period. Reasonable acceleration of industrial dispersion and urban decentralization would reduce materially the vulnerability of our industrial base to enemy attack.

STATE CONTROL OF CITIES [5]

A perplexed councilman of a city in upstate New York telephoned me not long ago to ask, "What kind of pipes will the state let us use for our city sewers?"

[5] From "The States Eclipse the Cities," article by Thomas C. Desmond, New York State Senator (Republican, Newburgh) and retired engineer. New York *Times Magazine.* p 14+. April 24, 1955. Reprinted by permission.

Although I am chairman of the New York State Senate Committee on Affairs of Cities, I was unaware that the state regulates sewer pipes. Since the question was solemnly put, I answered, just as solemnly, that I would look into it. Inquiries at several state agencies turned up a sanitary engineer who informed me that his bureau in the State Health Department most certainly does have the power to approve or veto the use of various types of pipes by cities.

This is one example—and not a far-fetched one—of how our states keep a tight, often choking rein on our cities in a variety of matters, from sewer pipes to tax rates, from bond issues to hiring a stenographer for the fire commissioner.

This year forty-six state legislatures have held or are holding sessions, and headlines in newspapers across the country have echoed charges and countercharges of state and city officials on the issue of state control of municipal affairs. The clash between the city's desire—and need—for more self-government and the state's attempt to retain its dominant position over the city has once more been brought to the fore as a major problem of government. It is a major problem because, although minor abuses by the states might be tolerated, when the states strangle local initiative, curb local responsibility, foist unnecessary expenses on local taxpayers and block new services needed in an age of urbanism, the cities have strong arguments for home rule.

What is the nature of the controls the states have over cities? How are they exercised? And what, specifically, are the results?

The controls are both legislative and administrative, and are applied and enforced in three ways. One is by passing laws that affect cities. Another is by judicial decisions. The third is by administrative curbs.

In theory the states can grant—or withhold—municipal home rule to any degree they wish. In practice they restrict home rule by enacting or not enacting laws—either special laws applying locally, or so-called general laws containing restrictive clauses aimed at certain cities. They can also do it by repealing or changing city charters. Like domineering mothers, the states refuse cities the right to run their own lives. Only twenty-one states make so much as a gesture toward granting some form of home rule to their cities, and even this is usually meaningless.

Thus, although cities have the right to elect their own officers and to carry out duties assigned to them by state legislatures, in most states they do not have the authority to determine their own form of government or the powers they may exercise. Many do not even have the right to choose which revenue sources they can tap to support local services.

The judicial form of control stems from the fact that the courts have repeatedly ruled against cities and for legislatures. Judges have denied cities any inherent right to self-government; cities are deemed the legal creatures of the state, with no powers except those granted by the state. Moreover, courts have ignored repeated evasions of constitutional prohibitions against laws applying to a single city.

As with legislative controls, so with administrative restrictions. States view the cities at best as irresponsible, unruly children capable of an amazing amount of mischief; therefore, they must be held to firm standards, if necessary by an occasional fiscal spanking. Today, nearly half the states force cities to follow state-prescribed budget systems and require periodic probes of city accounts, either by state agencies or state-approved accountants. The feeling is: spare the regulations and spoil the city.

States do aid cities in various ways. One is by providing technical assistance. For example, Joseph Watkins, a career personnel technician in the New York Civil Service Department, works in city halls throughout the state to help install modern personnel procedures. He also keeps a sharp eye out for violations of the merit system by job-hungry politicians. When such services are voluntarily accepted by the localities, neither local responsibility nor home rule is violated. But many states attempt to impose efficiency and virtue by restrictive state legislation which does more harm than good.

Another way states aid cities is by financial contributions. One out of every five dollars of the annual income of our cities comes from the states. But unfortunately the grants are usually hedged with many restrictions. Moreover, the cities must depend upon the real estate tax, a relic of the eighteenth century, for two out of every three tax dollars.

The states, viewing the cities as competitors for the taxpayer's dollar, not only force cities to rely on the property tax but also tightly limit the amount they can raise from this source. They have refused municipal pleas for the right to impose a payroll or an income tax, or to levy or increase taxes on local utilities— although the states themselves levy such taxes for state-wide use. This further shrinks the cities' tax base. In addition, legislatures often yield to pressure groups and pass laws that force cities to raise the salaries of some categories of employees or to take on other fiscal burdens.

Thus, city officials, trapped between expensive demands for airports, roads, hospitals, schools or salary increases, and inadequate funds to pay the bills, are today walking a perilous economic tightrope. Yet in all the quarrels between cities and states, the cities usually have to battle with both hands tied behind their backs.

The net result of these methods of state control is that our cities must beseech legislators for their basic right to exist, to govern, to police their streets, to provide water for their people. Unless they obtain legislative authorization from the states, they cannot establish parking lots, regulate intracity buses, stop slaughterhouses from opening up in residential areas, or do any of a thousand things a modern city must do for its people.

The city dweller who is the victim of the system may wonder how state controls became so thoroughly clamped on municipal affairs. One reason was the powerful position which the states assumed at the beginning of our national history. After the Revolution the states inherited all the authority formerly held by royal governors. At that time the legislatures dominated both the executive and judicial branches of the state governments. The Constitution later confirmed many of the powers the states had assumed under the Confederation. But, in those early years, the efforts of state control were not too onerous, for cities were small.

The cities' real troubles began with the growth of urbanism. As cities increased in size, political power passed from the farm to the tenement. The "city vote" became a prime target for ambitious politicians. Lawmakers discovered that more votes were usually to be gained by sponsoring local bills than by campaigning for even the most desirable state-wide legislation. (In all state capitols, local bills are passed or killed on the basis of "legislative courtesy." Customarily no bill affecting a city will be introduced or voted down without advance approval of the legislator representing that community.)

This has led to a seeming paradox. The short-changing of cities by states is traditionally attributed to over-representation of rural areas in our legislatures. Yet the rural representatives are by and large disinterested and do not mix in city affairs. The worst offenders in the strangulation of cities by states are legislators from the cities. In New York State, for example, forty-five out of fifty-eight state senators either live or work in cities.

In the course of time the growth of urban political power in the legislatures raised, in practice, the local legislative delegations to the position of superior governing bodies over the municipal officials. Without the approval of the local legislators the city authorities were unable to carry out needed programs. This proved especially troublesome when the legislative delegation was of one party and the municipal officials were of another, or when the delegation belonged to the minority party in the legislature.

In the resulting stalemates the failures of cities to plan in advance to meet clearly emerging problems of traffic congestion, slum clearance and crime has created a recurring series of emergencies. Clutching at any straw, the cities have often turned to the states for what aid they can get. In addition, weak local officials have often evaded responsibility and passed on to the states the solution of sensitive issues. All of these factors have tended to put and keep the state in the driver's seat.

What, more specifically, is wrong with this system of state control over cities? In what ways does it harm the cities?

It has been argued in behalf of the system that the cities have brought some of their woes upon themselves. That is true. Corruption has been no stranger in city halls. . . .

Yet cities are not as corrupt as some believe. William Embler, former Deputy Controller of New York State, informs me that the state's audit of the books of 8,000 localities every two years has disclosed remarkable official probity. Sums misappropriated in a recent year have totaled no more than $7,800.

The main thing wrong with the state control system is that cities are now too big and too complicated to have their affairs handled by outsiders who may not be as familiar as they should be with city problems.

Half our people now live in cities with populations of 100,000 or more. Our cities have become giant diversified businesses, operating airports, hospitals and water plants. They are often the largest employers in their respective regions. They need freedom to regulate their growth and the increasing physical and social problems caused by their size.

Our cities have gained maturity. But instead of recognizing what they can and must do for themselves, the states continue to pass laws interfering with them, often for reasons of spite. Legislators can punish opposing cliques, grant concessions and act as benign overlords or petty tyrants.

Another evil of the system is its waste of time and effort. Before my committee recently were bills to permit Poughkeepsie to sell some land it had acquired for hospital purposes and no longer needs, to authorize Ogdensburg to spend $5,000 on publicity, to let Newburgh turn over a dead-end street to a factory that needs it to expand. In some legislatures hundreds of local bills, of no concern to anyone except the single sponsor, must be considered and passed at each session.

Even when states, out of the best of motives, substitute arbitrary regulations for local flexibility, the end result is often waste and sometimes danger. Because cities are required to accept "the lowest responsible bid" when buying material, they must often purchase machinery from a distant source which cannot service it, rather than from a near-by source which can. There is no leeway, no discretion. Thus, some fire trucks in one city today carry different sets of hose connections to every fire because the lowest bidder on hose connections did not have connections to fit the fire hydrants in that city.

Another thing wrong with such strong state control is that lobbies can often use the state's power over cities to enrich themselves. For example, a bill was passed at the recent session of the New York Legislature to require cities to equip each fire truck with two sets of gas masks of a type apparently made by only a few manufacturers. . . .

What can be done to improve the state-city relationship? How can the cities gain some independence?

I do not propose that cities be cut loose to operate on their own. Local affairs are too intermingled with those of other levels of government for cities to become wholly autonomous. Arterial highways, control over courts, wage and hour regulations, annexation of land, war against communicable diseases—these are things which transcend local interest and call for state action. But if the delineation of state and local problems is difficult at times, it is hardly insuperable.

The standard should be this: what the states can do better than the cities should be done by the states; what the states and cities can do best together should be done jointly; what the cities can do better than the states should be done by the cities.

There remains the problem of how to achieve this method of operation. Professor Rodney Mott of Colgate University outlined for the American Municipal Association three conditions necessary to obtain home rule: (1) lively public support, (2) aggressive leadership by state leagues of municipalities, and (3) a change in the attitude of judges.

In rotary clubs and chambers of commerce, in women's clubs and welfare organizations, our people will have to voice demands that the states yield their authority over the cities. A rallying point could be a demand for the simple requirement that in every case where states force new expenses upon cities, the states would have to indicate how the expenses are to be met and authorize new tax levies if required. This would be a powerful influence in imposing a sense of responsibility on legislatures.

In states where the people have the right of initiative and referendum the voters can place freedom clauses in state constitutions which the lawmakers would not be able to skirt. In other states the campaign will have to be waged in constitutional conventions or by frontal attacks on the legislatures.

At future sessions bills should be introduced to provide that cities shall have all powers that legislatures are legally capable of granting to cities—subject to reasonable limitations. This would serve immediately to broaden the area of home rule. In addition, cities should be granted the power to draft and amend their own charters.

Not all public action, however, should be aimed at the states. The "buck-passers" on the local city councils who, when confronted with a politically hot issue, leave responsibility to the states, must be shown that the voters will not tolerate such supine behavior.

In the free association of cities the municipalities have opportunities to develop standards and employ experts without domination by the states. State leagues of municipalities need to be strengthened to bolster technical services available to cities and to withstand state intrusion. There is no basic need for conflict. The well-being of the states and cities depends upon the vitality and integrity of both.

But the best argument of all for home rule is the well-run city. Home rule should be earned by demonstrated capacity to govern. As long as graft and incompetence are found in city halls the states will have an excuse to justify their tight control over cities.

The American Municipal Association's "Credo of the American Mayor" states:

We believe that the principle of municipal independence carries with it the obligation to face our own problems, to meet our responsibilities, to finance our own enterprises within the limit of local resources and consistent with practical economic and social factors.

Here is expressed the spirit of responsibility which can win home rule and make it a means of progress.

PLANNING'S PLACE IN POLITICS [6]

Urban planning has a rich and colorful history. Over the past half-century immense strides have been made in dealing

[6] From "Some Political and Administrative Considerations in Urban Planning," article by Ernest A. Engelbert, associate professor, and Jess H. Walters, teaching assistant, Department of Political Science, University of California at Los Angeles. *Western City.* 31:56+. August 1955. Reprinted by permission.

particularly with the physical problems of urban growth. Yet despite the great gains that have been made urban planners have not succeeded in winning sufficient public acceptance and support for their work to enable them to keep abreast of the problems associated with the growth and dispersal of cities. . . .

Urban planning has not had a greater impact upon public policies because of the inadequacies in the political and administrative framework in which local planning is taking place. First of all some of the political and administrative approaches which have dominated urban planning have not been well-conceived or integrated. Second, urban planning has been viewed insufficiently as an intergovernmental function and process. And third, some of the current proposals for urban planning reform do not meet the basic conditions of political reality.

To a large extent the failure to develop a more adequate approach to urban analysis is due to the fact that there has not been a healthy working relationship between planners and political scientists. Urban planners have in general tried to develop their function as a technical science divorced from the political considerations of policy-making. This approach has led to a heavy emphasis upon physical planning. Where urban planners have consciously attempted to structure social and economic alternatives into their plans they have tried to do so independently of the political process. Political scientists on the other hand have approached the problems of city growth and planning largely from formal aspects of structure and organization. Few planning studies have dealt with the dynamics of the political decision-making process or the more substantive issues of public policy.

Partly as a result of these specialized professional approaches our understanding of urban planning as a political process has been limited in a number of ways:

(1) The development of a political theory of urbanism has been retarded. We do not possess an adequate philosophy of the role and place of the city in an evolving democracy of changing governmental and social institutions. Urban planners have been handicapped in devising plans to deal with urban concentration and dispersal because it is not clear what types of cities will most enhance the nation's development and welfare.

(2) The growth and spread of a metropolitan area is being assessed and planned too much in terms of the immediate metropolitan environment and local circumstances and insufficiently in terms of regional and interregional forces and influences. Urban planners are not always cognizant of the fact that regional factors may be more significant for planning in specific cities than any internal metropolitan factors.

(3) Insufficient attention is being given to some of the qualitative conditions of growth and change which take place in a community's economic and social structure, conditions which frequently are most determining in the technical design of a city in relation to its environs.

When viewed from the standpoint of intergovernmental relationships, urban planning is again at an extreme disadvantage. There are a great number of Federal and state functions, such as housing and home financing, highways, and military defense, which are important in determining the character and rate of urban dispersal, but there has in general been little consideration for the plans of specific cities in administering these functions. At the national level there has been no over-all review since 1937 of the impact of Federal functions upon cities. In California there is no agency at the state level concerned with the over-all problems of metropolitan planning, despite the most phenomenal urban growth rate of any state in the union. . . .

Urban planning will not be successful until it is viewed in the light of intergovernmental relationships and functions. The most wisely devised metropolitan plan will rest upon insecure foundations so long as major program decisions can be reached at Federal and state levels which are at variance with the planning objectives of a metropolitan area. Although there will be inevitable conflicts in the intergovernmental planning process, all governmental programs—Federal, state, and local—should be developed and oriented as far as possible to fit into the metropolitan regional plan.

Finally, planning for the metropolitan area has lagged because too much emphasis has been placed upon politically ineffectual solutions for improving the urban planning process. Because of local pride and vested interests, extensive local reorganization does not appear to be a feasible way for achieving more integrated urban planning. The whole history of annexations, consolidations, and other ways of modifying local government boundaries is not encouraging. Nor is it practicable to grant powers to cities to control urban sprawl beyond their borders in metropolitan areas where there is more than one incorporated community.

There is no single remedy which will serve as a political and administrative cure for the problems of metropolitan government. To marshal maximum political support urban planning must move forward along several fronts, local, state, and national.

The development of a regional plan covering the entire metropolitan area and adjacent land is the first step in controlling urban dispersal. Local constituencies cannot be expected to support any actions on an intergovernmental basis until the over-all objectives have been spelled out. The procedure recently set forth in the National Municipal League's "Model State and Regional Planning Law" is recommended.

Greater responsibility for urban planning needs to be assumed by state governments. The states are in a pivotal position not only because they are the sources of local powers, but they are likewise the instrumentalities through which a number of Federal programs are administered. Most of the states, however, need to set their own administrative houses in order to do this job adequately. In California, the Regional Planning Law should be amended to permit the state to exercise administrative and fiscal sanctions where local governments do not conform to an adopted regional plan.

At the national level a careful analysis of the impact of Federal programs upon metropolitan planning is urgently necessary. The recent reports of the Commission on Intergovernmental Relations gave at best only tangential attention to the problems arising from Federal activities in metropolitan areas. Either a major Federal agency such as the Housing and Home Finance Agency or a staff agency in the Executive Office of the President should be assigned the responsibility for continually assessing the consistency of Federal programs relating to urban areas. For the larger metropolitan areas consideration should be given to the creation of Federal inter-agency metropolitan committees to cooperate with urban planners in keeping Federal programs in harmony with local plans.

Last, but not least, the administrative organization for planning at the local levels should be designed to integrate the staff functions of planning with policy-making and operational functions of government. The planning process should be merged with the political process as much as possible in local policy formulation and decision-making. Urban planning should be regarded not simply as a city or area problem but as a process which affects all phases of national welfare.

VII. PUBLIC PARTICIPATION

EDITOR'S INTRODUCTION

As with most other governmental or quasi-governmental undertakings, community planning can be only as successful as its support by the general public permits it to be. Over the past half century, there have been many instances where elaborate plans for major cities, ignored or opposed by the general public, have never been put into effect. Decades later, the same plans with a few revisions, but now supported by an alerted citizenry, have become alive and meaningful.

Unlike police or health regulations, planning usually cannot be put into effect by simple law enforcement. It requires public knowledge and continued public enthusiasm. This final section deals with a variety of ways in which such support and enthusiasm can be expressed—through the leadership of public utilities, through a "civic approach" in which all private groups subordinate their own special interests for the public good, and through the neighborhood-by-neighborhood approach recommended by a new, privately sponsored group known as ACTION (American Council To Improve Our Neighborhoods).

Through these and other means, the American people are learning the economic, social, and moral values of planning our communities to meet commonly desired objectives.

PUBLIC UTILITY LEADERSHIP [1]

If you happened to be in the Hotel Marion, Little Rock [Arkansas] one day in November you would have been aroused from a noonday nap by tremendous applause. More than five hundred citizens from all but a few of the seventy-five counties and representing the top drawer of business, education, and the professions, were on their feet not once but twice. They were

[1]From "Arkansas Reaping Benefits from Ham Moses' Big 'Plan,'" article. *Manufacturers Record.* 123:52-3+. December 1954. Reprinted by permission.

giving a spontaneous endorsement to their long recognized leader. C. Hamilton Moses had sketched for them a ten-year plan, "not a prophecy—not guess work—but a realistic assessment of where we are going by 1965."

He foresaw the [Arkansas] population of 2 million with a per capita income of $1,750. Moses forecast retail sales of $3 billion—just about double today's sales—and cash farm income of $825 million, up 50 per cent. Manufacturing jobs would go up to 110,000, predicted Moses, as he cited other optimistic forecasts for ten years ahead. Along with these business statistics he predicted an increase in per pupil expenditures in the schools from $127 in 1955 to $250 in 1965.

Moses told his audience that Arkansas' days of losing population are past; that its location and resources and assets would make the next decade the state's greatest—IF. Behind this single reservation was Moses' request that the membership of the Arkansas Economic Council go on record in favor of a program that would assure these goals.

It was not his first time to plead for their support, but Moses indicated it might be the last. He was reelected president of the Economic Council, a statewide leadership group with some 1,400 members. (Moses has been president since it was organized in 1943 to make sure there was a job for every returning serviceman.)

And behind his eloquent appeal was a record equaled by few living men. President of Arkansas Power and Light Company, 1941-1952, Moses as board chairman has devoted almost full time to the "Arkansas Plan," a label that embraces one of the broadest and most unusual programs of economic and area development in the nation. Backing him up is AP&L President R. E. Ritchie, who heads the Pulaski County Citizens Council, a development group in metropolitan Little Rock. In addition, Vice President W. M. Shepherd directs the company's development program and serves as chairman of the state's Industrial Development Committee.

The Arkansas story is one of the romances of not only the electric industry, but the entire field in which communities and citizens have undertaken to develop themselves and provide their own future. Fundamental to the "Arkansas Plan" is the philosophy of individual freedom under which people are responsible for their own welfare and future.

In ten years, the Economic Council has held more than one thousand meetings in three hundred communities to stir up enthusiasm and inspire people to do their own jobs of development and improvement. Some five hundred organizations on the home-town level, representing some 100,000 people, have had some part in the development work in the towns and rural sections.

Just what is there for all of these people to do? What motivates them to give up their leisure time to work for the community? This answer reveals the genius of the "Arkansas Plan."

It is not the public relations program of a power company nor the calculated plan of a government agency. Nor is it a program proposed by business or the farmer, or education, or labor. It crosses all of these lines and is bipartisan and is accepted by all these groups.

One thing that makes the Arkansas team doubly effective is that it is joined in wholeheartedly by both the state government and citizen organizations. Industrial development projects generally are joint undertakings of the Resources and Development Commission, a state agency, the Arkansas Economic Council, and a number of the larger industries. Another underlying principle is the attitude and policy of the power company. Its interest is admittedly "enlightened selfishness" but the company doesn't try to put itself in front of the crowd. . . .

There is nothing spectacular about the various programs aimed at industrial, area and rural improvement. There is a minimum of drum beating and advertising so often connected with this sort of thing. Take community development work. It's cosponsored by AP&L, the Economic Council and the Resources & Development Commission. Community counselors, trained men who know how to work with community leaders and how to organize them into action, devote full time to contact work. Two men are provided by the power company, one each by the other agencies. They get citizens interested primarily through what is called a community clinic. This is a town forum. Citizens are invited in groups of less than forty to attend an open meeting that lasts one hour. Every citizen gets a chance to air his views, ideas, complaints about "what our town ought to do."

Counselors are on the road nearly all the time either conducting clinics or keeping alive the enthusiasm generated by these meetings. After each clinic session, citizens fill out a questionnaire listing their recommendations for community projects. After the series of clinics is over the counselor recaps the information contained in the cards. This is put together in what is called an analysis and returned to the sponsoring group and community leaders. From the analysis the community has a "people's plan." This isn't the documentation of experts nor of a visiting specialist. It is a consensus of the local citizenship. On the clinic card each citizen has indicated whether or not he is willing to work for the projects agreed upon by the community. Every community can arrive at its own program which already has popular support.

No one pretends that the clinic itself has accomplished any projects. It is a forum and sounding board. Counselors don't stop on paper. In many communities it is necessary to organize a community development council. This is a sort of city council at large. It is made up of the officers and representatives of all organized groups—civic clubs, churches, veterans, labor, farm and women's clubs. In some cities chambers of commerce handle the job.

What helps keep the program alive year after year—124 communities were active in 1953—is a contest among towns. AP&L puts up $4,800 in prize money for winners in the Community Accomplishment Contest. Five communities in three population groups are selected for their accomplishments. Their leaders receive the prize money at an annual awards dinner.

Top community in 1953 in the 4,001-20,000 population class was Brinkley, an agriculture center in the East Arkansas rice belt. For years the community had worked to get an industry which would provide jobs for farm labor displaced by machines. Industrialists came, took a look, and went away never to return. Brinkley just wasn't ready. In 1948 Brinkley heard of the "Arkansas Plan" and asked the sponsors to conduct a community clinic. During the clinic Brinkley civic leaders learned that local citizens were aware of the community's problems and anxious to work on them. A community development council was organized and when the first Community Accomplishment Contest was held in 1950 Brinkley was quick to enter and proud indeed to be awarded second prize. Each year produced a finer town and when in 1953 the Phillips-Jones Corporation, makers of the nationally known Van Heusen shirt, came to town looking for a suitable location, Brinkley *was* ready. The years of community building paid off. A new fifty-bed hospital, new schools, miles of new pavement, and numerous other improvements were evidence enough to this manufacturer of the fine and friendly attitude of this community. . . .

First place in the smallest population group (1,000 and under) went to Decatur (population 350), a mountain community in the Ozarks of northwest Arkansas. Here is what the judges found in its first place scrapbook for 1953: $3,000 improvement in the water system; a new sewer system; new whiteway lighting; $5,000 airport; a new city lake and swimming pool; $8,500 improvement to streets; general improvements to churches, schools, commercial and residential buildings, and a ball park constructed for $13,000. In addition, community leaders set up their own industrial fund of $245,000, put up a building and leased it for ten years to a packing company. This increased jobs 100 per cent overnight.

There is a good deal of pencil work connected with the programs. AP&L helps with this, too, supplying industrial survey forms to committees and helping communities get together information. Through the Economic Council and the cooperation of the University of Arkansas there is a continuing program of research. Key committees work on such basic problems as taxation, industrial development, marketing, tourist development, health and welfare, and land use. On some of the critical problems like taxation and industrial development the University has undertaken studies which provide the information to help solve these problems.

The "Arkansas Plan" doesn't stop at the city limits. In fact, there are more contests and citizenship programs for the rural people. With a greater area and more settlements, the Rural Community Improvement Program in three years has already passed the number of communities which take part in the city contest. Rural Community Improvement is a contest jointly sponsored by AP&L with the Agriculture Extension Service and the Arkansas Press Association.

You would expect the Arkansas sponsors in general, and AP&L in particular, to be sold on their "Arkansas Plan." But this program has attracted the attention of the nation and weathered the acid tests of editors and writers for *Fortune, The American, Time, Business Week,* and the *Reader's Digest. . . .* William Hard, the *Digest's* roving editor, concludes: "For getting this country reconverted to local, individual cooperative effort, I would welcome a whole army of such Rebels as . . . [Hamilton Moses]."

THE "CIVIC APPROACH" IN PITTSBURGH [2]

The Pittsburgh story is basically the planning and carrying forward of a broad program of regional improvement and development. Within a period of seven years, there has been invested or committed to be invested in the Pittsburgh area, . . . [about $1.6 billion] of private and public money. The program consists of such improvements as a new airport, five skyscrapers, a steel mill capable of producing two million tons of steel annually, public off-street parking facilities, new parks (city and state), a smoke abatement program, dams for flood control, stream purification, slum clearance, public housing, a new hotel, new downtown apartments, a multi-million dollar highway program, and an expansion of educational institutions.

Why this vitality? What caused a city sliding down hill so fast to suddenly be propelled upwards at a breath-taking rate?

[2] From "Citizens' Responsibility for Civic Planning—The Pittsburgh Story," address by Theodore L. Hazlett, Jr., solicitor. Allegheny Conference on Community Development, delivered before the Citizens Planning Conference, Columbus, Ohio, May 19, 1954. In *American Planning and Civic Annual, 1954.* American Planning and Civic Association. Washington, D.C. 1954. p 186-94. Reprinted by permission.

The reasons, of course, are many—chance, good planning, and availability of private and public monies. Underlying them all, however, I personally feel that the results were accomplished by a change of attitude in Pittsburgh by Pittsburghers. . . . Not too long ago, a resident of Pittsburgh was apt to be somewhat defensive about his home town, parrying the remarks about the smoky city with some such retort as, "Well it may not be the best place in which to live, but it certainly is a good place to make money." Today, the average Pittsburgher speaks with pride about his city and is delighted to have an opportunity to discuss, usually at the request of outsiders, the Pittsburgh of the present. . . .

The change of attitude was a complete rearrangement of basic ideas and behavior patterns. Such can occur only in periods of crisis, and at the end of the war years the city found itself in that position. Pittsburgh was dying, if not dead. Assessed valuations had dropped radically. Industry was moving away. One reason given was the inability to attract managerial talent to the area. The men were willing, provided salaries were high enough, but their wives objected. With the dropping of industrial values, commercial and residential values also fell. The future was as dark as the soot laden air. The change of attitude was simply this. The community realized that a new approach was necessary; that in order to revitalize a city, certain problem areas had to be staked out and eliminated by cooperative effort on the part of all segments of the community, and also, by farsighted rather than by expedient thinking that is so often prevalent in the normal political and business world. This approach I call the *Civic Approach*. I can explain it more clearly, I think, by showing it to you in actual operation.

The fundamental project and the foundation upon which the Pittsburgh improvement program was built was smoke abatement. It was realized in the very beginning that excessive smoke and the unfavorable reputation it gave the city were major obstacles to the community's future growth. In 1941, the Council of the City of Pittsburgh passed a Smoke Control Ordinance, but enforcement was deferred, because of the war conditions, until October 1, 1946 when it was made effective for industry and

railroads. A year later, residential properties within the city were
brought under its control. The essence of the Pittsburgh ordinance is tackling smoke at the root or the problem by stopping
smoke at its source. The methods have been the use of smokeless
fuel . . . and also the installation and use of modern mechanical
firing equipment for both industrial and domestic uses. The
results have been startling. Official figures of the United States
Weather Bureau show that Pittsburgh now gets about 69 per cent
more sunshine. In seven years, 1946 to 1952, the hours of total
smoke have been reduced by more than 69 per cent, heavy smoke
hours by 93 per cent. Cleaner living conditions have saved city
residents an estimated $27 million annually, or $41 each
in laundry and cleaning bills, household expenses and other
economies. . . .

Looking at the change in thinking of the business community, two examples immediately come to . . . mind. The heart
of the city of Pittsburgh is that area known as the Golden
Triangle. It consists of approximately four hundred acres and is
bounded on two sides by rivers, the Allegheny and the Mononga-
hela, which form at their juncture, the Ohio, and on the third
by a sudden rise of land. This is the city's most expensive commercial area. There has been historically a rivalry between the
business interests in the upper part of the Triangle and those in
the lower half, a condition which is prevalent in most cities.
It has in the past had some very bitter moments, and yet, when
the redevelopment of the lower part of the Triangle was being
planned, the business community united. Mr. Edgar J. Kaufmann, President of the Kaufmann's Department Store, serving
as a member of the Urban Redevelopment Authority of Pittsburgh, gave unstintingly of his efforts to pursuade the Equitable
Society to become the redeveloper of the area. His store is
located in the uptown area and is the biggest department store
in the city. One of his closest competitors is the Joseph Horne
store located in the downtown area, and immediately adjoining
the redevelopment area. This redevelopment brought a new life
into that lower area, and guaranteed and preserved its values for
many, many years to come. This in my opinion was . . . the civic

approach and action—it was thinking on the broader scope, not the narrow expedient scope.

Newspapers, radio and television play, as we all know, a very important part in shaping public opinion in our communities. In Pittsburgh, not only have they been friendly, but they have taken an active role in the improvement program. One newspaper has assigned a special reporter to this field who spends most of his time developing the stories relating to the program. Others have at least one or two men on their staff who also keep abreast and fully informed of the progress that is being made, and the relationship of one matter to another, which is of utmost importance. Accurate reporting is a necessity, but it is particularly important in the civic field, so that the community can fairly appraise the program and motives of those proposing change. Any change is generally resisted. The people ought to know, and are entitled to know, the full background so as to intelligently appraise the matter. . . . Without cooperation of the news agencies in the Pittsburgh area, the Pittsburgh program would never have been accomplished. They too have a new approach— the *Civic Approach*.

Another aspect about this new approach is the citizen's desire and willingness to serve. Hundreds of persons have taken part in the program. They have participated without monetary compensation on committees and counsels, and have given freely of their time and talents to solving the community's problems. A list of such activities would fill several pages, but here are just a few: The Citizens' Airport Committee; the Citizens' Committee on Mass Transportation; Mayor's Emergency Traffic Committee; United Smoke Council; Recreation, Conservation and Park Council; Mayor's Water Committee; Point Park Committee; and Mayor's Committee for a Greater City. Through the use of such committees, there is made available to public officials, the very best experience that the city has to offer, experience which could not be bought, and on the other side of the coin, the citizen himself, through his constructive and unselfish work, receives a feeling of satisfaction that is also immeasurable.

This changing attitude, in all its ramifications did not occur over night—it was a long process. It was nurtured by an organization called the Allegheny Conference on Community Development. This group was the catalyst in the picture. It is a private nonprofit organization serving as an over-all civic agency, stimulating and coordinating research and planning. Its objective is to assure the well being and growth of the Allegheny region as a well adjusted, healthy community capable of providing its citizens with conditions essential to good living. The governing body of the Conference is a citizens' sponsoring committee consisting of, at the present time, seventy-two persons from the field of industry, commerce, finance, labor, education, public administration, newspaper and radio, and civic affairs. . . .

How much does it cost to run such an organization? On an annual basis, the budget of the conference during the past years is roughly around $88,000. Where does the money come from? For the most part, the money is raised by public subscription, by the Pittsburgh Civic Business Council. This council is a central fund raising agency providing for the regular budgets of the Allegheny Conference, the Chamber of Commerce, the Pittsburgh Convention Bureau, and the Better Business Bureau. It is the community fund idea being applied to these civic types of organizations. Although the conference is affiliated with the council, it fully retains its freedom of action, its own individual identity, and operating economy. The conference also receives special grants of money for special projects. . . .

That in brief is the basic organization of the conference. . . . In what manner does the Conference function? . . . First and foremost, the Conference is a planning and research agency. It takes unto itself a specific community problem, develops the relevant facts, and then suggests a possible remedy or remedies. A good example of such is the off-street parking study. . . .

Another category is that of dissemination of information. The conference makes available its planning and research reports to the general public and to those who are vitally affected or interested. The list of brochures, pamphlets, and articles, published by the conference in recent years runs well over one hundred and fifty items. Just recently, on behalf of the county smoke control program, one hundred and ten thousand pamphlets describing this program and informing the people as to the requirements that have to be met by residential owners were distributed through the county school systems and information was also given to the teachers in the schools so that they could hold classes on the problem and explain it to the children who in turn would carry the information home to the parents.

A third method is obtaining cooperative effort and acting also in certain cases as an arbitrator. . . . [As an illustration] part of our improvement program of the city is the construction of a limited access highway cutting right through the middle of our community which will take the east-west traffic through the city in a very short period of time as compared to the long and difficult trip that it now is. One of the properties that had to be acquired as the highway approached the center of the city is owned by the Baltimore and Ohio Railroad Company, and it meant the relocation of many of their tracks and also the acquisition of their existing station. This is a state program and the state highway engineers began several years ago to discuss with the officials of the Baltimore and Ohio Railroad, the question which is always involved, and that is "How much should the railroad get for its property?" After several years of negotiation, it became critical that a decision be reached because of the delay which would be created in the highway construction program. The conference, feeling the need that there be no delay, offered to come into the picture to act, in the sense, as an arbitrator. It listened to arguments on both sides, made its own appraisal of the situation, and recommended terms of a settlement agreement. Both parties accepted this agreement, and our highway program is moving according to schedule. This important aspect of obtaining cooperation between parties should not be overlooked as the area in which an organization such as the conference . . . can be effective. In many of these projects it requires approvals of one sort or another, and agreements between all three levels of government, Federal, state and local, and even within the local scene you have a county government, a city government, a borough government or township government that is affected. In Pittsburgh we have a great number of smaller governmental units, and . . . providing these parties a place in which to meet to discuss their program and their problems in an atmosphere of fairness and impartiality, has proved invaluable to the Pittsburgh program.

The conference also functions very effectively as a "gadfly." This is the technique used to get these programs off the drawing boards into actual construction and finished. Once the conference makes the plan and gets the agency created that is to carry it out, it then doesn't sit back and do nothing more. Rather it acts as an expediter; it acts as a pin pricker, it offers constructive criticism, and assists wherever it can. Its Executive Director and staff serve on special technical committees. Its prime job, though, is to see that plans are carried out. Many of these projects take a long period of time for their completion. For example—in any state highway program—if you do not have an agency in the community looking out for the community's interest, making sure that the state highway program moves along on schedule, many times these programs never are carried to completion for many, many years, if ever.

Lastly, there is a development in the Pittsburgh scene which is not duplicated nor could it be duplicated, I'm afraid, in many cities. That is the administration of private monies for public uses. In Pittsburgh, we are benefited with a large number of very wealthy foundations, whose trustees are devoted to the city and wish to see it improved in whatever manner it can be. These trustees, rather than giving the money directly to the city, will give it to the conference and the conference will act as the administrator of the expenditure of the money. Here is how it works. A foundation of the city, the Sarah Mellon Scaife Foundation desired to give the city a children's zoo. The money for the zoo was given to the conference. The conference had architects prepare working drawings and specifications which were approved by the city officials interested such as the Director of the Department of Parks and Recreation, and then the conference took bids on the work and with permission of the city had its contractor go upon public property and build thereon the zoo. It then formally dedicated the zoo to the citizens and people of Pittsburgh.

That briefly is the Pittsburgh story. It of course is not the whole story, but the last chapters have not as yet been writ-

ten. . . . Our cities are a priceless heritage, they must be con-
served, beautified and improved. They mirror the soundness of
our democratic institutions. Let us make sure through unselfish
citizen participation that the image is true and one in which we
may take pride.

ACTION FOR YOUR COMMUNITY [3]

Recently a housing expert, visiting a city of 40,000 people,
was asked by the high school social studies teacher to talk to her
students about slums—they were studying Housing in America.
"Our town doesn't have any slums," she said, "so my students
are completely ignorant of the problem."

Next day, the housing expert came to the class armed with
some startling facts. In their "slumless city," he told them, 25
per cent of the homes had no indoor bathtubs or bathing facilities, 21 per cent had outside toilets or privies, 9 per cent had no
running water, 26 per cent no central heating. One tenement
housing sixteen families used three outside toilets half a block
away.

Perhaps those boys and girls had never thought of the miserable shacks on the other side of town as slums, or the overcrowded mansions-turned-rooming-houses on what was once a
fine old street as a blighted area. In preparation for their next
class, the housing expert suggested a tour of the city to find out
about housing conditions in their own home town.

Like practically every community in the country, large or
small, this city had slums and run-down areas, which were slowly
eating away at its good neighborhoods. But, like this teacher and
her conscientious students, too many people are ignorant of the
facts. It's easy to avoid driving through that part of town, pleas-
anter to look the other way. Or worse yet, we become used to
the dilapidated houses, the decaying neighborhoods. We hardly
see them.

But slums need looking at, for they are like a contagious disease. Every day we read in the newspapers about a wave of teen-

[3] From "It's Time for ACTION," article by Major General Frederick A. Irving (Retired), president, the American Council To Improve Our Neighborhoods.
Parents' Magazine. 31:54+. March 1956. Reprinted by permission.

age knifings, a fatal tenement fire, an epidemic of diphtheria, an infant dead from rat bite—these are the earmarks of the slums. Even if there were no humanitarian, religious or ethical motives for removing these eye-sores from our communities, there would still be compelling economic reasons. America cannot afford slums. Many of your tax dollars go to subsidize the community services which slum areas require. You cannot afford slums. Your money is at stake, also your health, your well-being. Disease breeds in slums. Crime festers there. Delinquency stems from there. And disease and crime, delinquency and vice, stretch their tentacles far out from the slums themselves.

Several years ago, the frightening speed with which slums were developing in urban areas throughout the country became the deep concern of many leaders in the housing field. In 1953 they met in a series of round table discussions to consider what could be done to stem the tide of decay. A task force was appointed to gather facts and opinions from leaders in labor, education, religion, public service, industry, civic organizations.

The reports came back—agreement that a national nonprofit, nonpartisan organization could greatly encourage local action in clearing up local conditions. The American Council To Improve Our Neighborhoods, or ACTION, as it is known by its initials was launched in the nation's capital on November 15, 1954. President Eisenhower, who was on hand to address ACTION's inaugural gathering, placed the group's aims high on the urgent category of national public service projects. He said it "seems to represent to me much more emphatically than do most groups almost the philosophy of government by which I live."

Because public apathy, neglect and loss of pride in our homes has often permitted slum conditions to creep in, ACTION has undertaken, as its first step, an information program to change these attitudes. The Advertising Council, the public service agency of the advertising industry, has undertaken a nation-wide campaign on behalf of ACTION to get the message across. These are some of the startling facts they are bringing home to America.

1. One out of every ten nonfarm homes has slipped into decay and become a threat to the well-being of the community.

2. Twenty million houses urgently need repairs and basic improvements.

3. Less than half of the homes across the nation are in what we could call "good" condition.

At this point, you may shrug your shoulders in the happy knowledge that at least your own property shows no blight and that your neighborhood is free from the menace of the slum.

But don't be too complacent. If there is no blight in your neighborhood, you may find it in the next one. It may be an old residential quarter of very fine houses with an illustrious past. Old houses can mellow with age on quiet streets shaded by trees. Or they can rot as the paint peels off, the roof leaks and the whole neighborhood—parks, schools, as well as houses—becomes less desirable.

"Well," you say, "it isn't threatening me right now. And even if worse comes to worst, if things do begin to run down, I can always move away."

And so you can, if you are willing to pay the cost. You will break ties with old friends and neighbors. You may travel farther, and at greater cost, to get to work. And when you try to sell your old house, you may find that its value has already dropped.

And in your new home, have you really escaped the problem? Or have you learned that no home is an island, that every home and every individual is bound up with the community?

The only way you can stop slums and housing decay is to fight them.

And ACTION is there to help you. One of ACTION's primary functions is preparing material to help you formulate and carry out an effective local program to prevent trouble before it starts. It can bring you the benefit of other group experiences and supply you with technical information whether you are a property owner, builder, member of a civic group or a city official.

The example of what other communities are doing may help you. For instance, in the area known as "The Back-of-the-Yards" in Chicago, much of the housing is fifty to seventy-five years old and evidences of deterioration were widespread—sagging roofs and porches, peeling paint, crumbling foundations and general wear and tear. A citizens' group that calls itself the Back-of-the-Yards Neighborhood Council called together some influential people in the area. Together they mapped out a conservation program. Money for home modernization loans was made available by the local banks who also agreed to issue mortgages on new homes. Within ten months one out of every eight homes had been improved in some way. Stores that had been standing vacant were converted into dwellings and five of the empty lots in the community were set aside for public playgrounds. Now new houses are going up on other empty lots—a sure sign of a healthy neighborhood.

In another Chicago area there is a block of small apartment buildings, many of them cooperatively owned. They face a small park which back in 1949 was going to rack and ruin. Grass and plants had become a jungle. The broken bottles tossed into the park lay where they fell, a constant hazard to youngsters. Older children began to commit petty acts of property destruction, while inadequate street lighting encouraged night prowlers and criminals. One building on the block was sold to a real estate speculator who rented a room apiece to families. The place became a breeding ground for rats and vermin.

Then the residents heard of the area's Hyde Park-Kenwood Community Conference and with the help of this organization got together and formed the Sycamore Block group. After airing their gripes at several evening sessions, they set up standards and committees to carry out several immediate goals—park improvement, street lighting and a traffic light at a busy intersection.

Once the city realized that residents were interested and determined, park maintenance picked up and the city installed additional lights. Encouraged by their initial successes, the people next went after increased police control and elimination of illegal truck parking. The children were invited to tackle the problem of keeping trash off the lawns.

It took over a year of investigations and court cases to correct the one-room-to-a-family situation in the overcrowded apartment house, but violations were finally corrected and the forces of decay were reversed.

These are two cases but there are many others the country over. . . .

Do these sound like emergency measures? In many cases they are. But it is better yet if the emergency never occurs. Be alert. Be vigilant. Don't let your neighborhood slip toward decay. The way to prevent this is to get together with your neighbors for action. Study the problem. Know what needs to be done.

Start out by taking an inventory of the tools you have to work with:

Is there a workable, over-all plan for the community's development?

Are the uses of land well directed and controlled by a zoning ordinance?

Are there codes to insure minimum housing standards for health, fire prevention, building safety?

Has your community adopted a long range capital improvement budget to provide the facilities it needs—from a branch library to a health clinic, sewage treatment plant or an expressway?

Such things are not ends in themselves, but they are good tools for reaching desirable goals.

Then talk with your neighbors and find out how they feel about the neighborhood. Do they think the streets are safe, quiet and clean? Do they wish there were more parks? Are they worried because the school is overcrowded? And do they feel that these problems are important enough to do something about?

Settle on a clear-cut goal you all think worth fighting for. You may not be able to get everyone in at the start. Begin with those who feel interested enough to do something. The others will come along later.

Effective action must be thoughtful and well-planned. Facts are essential. If they have not already been collected, a preliminary fact-finding study can well be the group's first major project. City and county offices are important sources of information. Try to establish a good working relationship with someone in each main department. They can give you information on such things as the number of zoning exceptions granted each year, the cost of public services in a particular district, the number and kinds of housing conversions, the amount of park area or playground space, or on assessed valuations.

There are countless other possible sources for special kinds of information: the librarian, banks, real estate boards, the chamber of commerce, local utilities, the council of social agencies, newspaper editors. They will answer your questions or will lead you to others for the facts you need.

After your group is organized and armed with facts, it is ready to develop its program and to act. If you are new to this sort of thing, test your strength on a short-term goal—maybe just a clean-up campaign in one block or better street lighting. One success can breed another.

So the most important thing is to get started—know your local problems, set realistic objectives and act. ACTION will be glad to assist you with specific suggestions and literature. (Write to them at Box 462 Radio City Station, New York 20, New York.) But only action on your part can really do the job.

YOUR COMMUNITY'S PLAN—HOW GOOD IS IT? [4]

No master plan is any better than the information, the thought and the imagination that have gone into it.

Those are hard qualities to judge, yet you can get an idea of how good your town's master plan is simply by asking four practical questions:

Is the plan big enough? Most towns are growing faster outside the city limits than within them. It doesn't do much good to plan inside the boundary, only to have chaos take over at the city line.

One planning authority, Professor Christopher Tunnard of Yale, views the six-hundred-mile stretch from Norfolk, Virginia, to Portland, Maine, as one continuous city, to be planned as a unit.

[4] "How Good Is Your Town's Master Plan?" article. *Changing Times,* the Kiplinger magazine. 9:24. September 1955. Reprinted by permission.

Your town's planning need not be that all-embracing. But it should at least be developed in cooperation with adjoining townships or as part of a county-wide pattern.

Does it show vision? The most famous planning dictum of all is Daniel Burnham's "Make no little plans; they have no magic to stir men's blood."

Farsightedness certainly is a major virtue in planning. The heavily traveled expressway along Manhattan's East Side was ridiculed when first proposed. So was the Congress Street expressway in Burnham's 1909 plan for Chicago. Yet this super-street, badly needed today, is now under construction.

So if you find farsighted, exciting concepts in your town's master plan, you probably have a worthwhile plan.

Is it flexible? No plan ever is finished. Cities change constantly. Each change generates other changes.

A street is extended and becomes a popular traffic channel. The traffic attracts businesses. The street also makes undeveloped land accessible. The landowners subdivide. New houses spring up. Then need arises for new schools, a new fire station, more water, bigger sewers, better bus service. That evokes more planning, which begets more changes.

Your town should have a permanent planning agency to make planning a continuous process.

Is it enforced? The final test is whether the plan is working. If any landowner can fly in the face of the plan simply by asking the zoning board for a spot exception to the zoning regulations, your plan isn't worth what it costs. Your plan is working only if your local officials make it stick.

BIBLIOGRAPHY

An asterisk (*) preceding a reference indicates that the article or a part of it has been reprinted in this book.

BOOKS AND PAMPHLETS

American Automobile Association. Parking problems. 200p. The Association. 1712 G St., N.W. Washington 6, D.C. '55.

American Council To Improve Our Neighborhoods. ACTION—a long range program for a better America. 18p. The Council. Box 462, Radio City Station. New York 20. '55.

American Council To Improve Our Neighborhoods. Time for action. 31p. The Council. Box 462, Radio City Station. New York 20. '55.

Association of State Planning and Development Agencies. National forum on planning and development problems and techniques; proceedings, tenth annual convention, June 7-10, 1955, Denver, Colorado. 176p. The Association. 1026 17th St., N.W. Washington 6, D.C. '55.

*Bartholomew, Harland. Development and planning of American cities. (Carnegie press occasional papers no 1) 26p. Carnegie Institute of Technology. Pittsburgh, Pa. '50.

Bartholomew, Harland. Land use in American cities. 196p. Harvard University Press. Cambridge, Mass. '55.

Breese, Gerald and Whiteman, D. E. Approach to urban planning. 147p. Princeton University Press. Princeton, N.J. '53.

Burton, Hal. City fights back. 318p. Citadel Press. New York. '54.

Caplow, Theodore. City planning. 22p. Burgess Publishing Company. 426 So. 6th St. Minneapolis 15, Minn. '50.

Chamber of Commerce of the United States. Brighter future for America's cities. 149p. The Chamber. Washington 6, D.C. '55.

Chamber of Commerce of the United States. Construction and Civic Development Department. Urban development guidebook. 102p. The Chamber. Washington 6, D.C. '55.

Colean, M. L. Renewing our cities. 181p. Twentieth Century Fund. New York. '53.

Gallion, A. B. Urban pattern: city planning and design. 446p. D. Van Nostrand Co. New York. '50.

Holberg, O. G. Exploring the small community. 199p. University of Nebraska Press. Lincoln 8, Neb. '55.

Hoover, R. C. and Perry, E. L. Church and city planning. (Survey guide no2) 36p. National Council of the Churches of Christ in the U.S.A. 297 Fourth Ave. New York 10. '55.

Howard, Ebenezer. Garden cities of tomorrow. 167p. S. Sonnenschein &
co. London. '02.
    Second ed. of Tomorrow: a peaceful path to real reform.
Howard, Ebenezer. Tomorrow: a peaceful path to real reform. 176p.
S. Sonnenschein & co. London. 1898.
International Congresses for Modern Architecture. Heart of the city;
towards the humanization of urban life. 185p. Farrar, Strauss. New
York. '52.
*James, Harlean, ed. American planning and civic annual, 1951. 150p.
American Planning and Civic Association. 901 Union Trust Build-
ing. Washington 5, D.C. '52.
    Reprinted in this book: Bartholomew, Harland. The plan—its prepara-
ration, composition and form. p97-102.
*James, Harlean, ed. American planning and civic annual, 1954. 211p.
American Planning and Civic Association. 901 Union Trust Build-
ing. Washington 5, D.C. '54.
    Reprinted in this book: Hazlett, T. L., Jr. Citizens' responsibility for
civic planning; the Pittsburgh story. p 186-94.
*Kyle, Lyle C. Planning your community. (Citizen's pamphlet series
no 16) 23p. Governmental Research Center. University of Kansas.
Lawrence, Kan. '55.
Lee, R. H. The city: urbanism and urbanization in major world regions.
568p. J. B. Lippincott. Philadelphia. '55.
Miller, H. V. Mr. planning commissioner. 81p. Public Administration
Service. Chicago. '54.
Mumford, Lewis. Culture of cities. 586p. Harcourt, Brace & Co. New
York. '38.
    A "classic" in the planning field.
National Municipal League. Model state and regional planning law. 66p.
The League. 47 E. 68th St. New York 21. '55.
National Recreation Association. Recreation for your community. 15p.
The Association. 8 W. 8th St. New York 11. '54.
New York State. Department of Commerce. Local planning and zoning.
83p. The Department. Albany, N.Y. '53.
Orlans, Harold. Utopia, ltd. 313p. Yale University Press. New Haven,
Conn. '53.
Ridley, C. E. and others. Municipal year book, 1955. 588p. Interna-
tional City Managers' Association. 1313 E. 60th St. Chicago 37.
'55.
Rodwin, Lloyd. British New Towns policy. 252p. Harvard University
Press. Cambridge, Mass. '56.
Segoe, Laidlas. Local planning administration. 337p. International City
Managers' Association. 1313 E. 60th St. Chicago 37. '48.
Sert, J. L. Can our cities survive? an ABC of urban problems, their
analysis, their solutions, based on the proposals formulated by the
CIAM [International Congresses for Modern Architecture]. 259p.
Harvard University Press. Cambridge, Mass. '42.

Shaw, Frederick. American city. 92p. Oxford Book Company 222 Fourth Ave. New York 3. '53.

Spectorsky, A. C. Exurbanites. 278p. J. B. Lippincott. Philadelphia. '55.
    A satirical commentary on the exurbs, the author's word for the areas beyond the suburbs.

Stein, C. S. Toward New Towns for America. 245p. University Press of Liverpool. Liverpool, England. '51.

Tunnard, Christopher. City of man. 424p. Charles Scribner's Sons. New York. '53.

*United States. Commission on Intergovernmental Relations. Report to the President for transmittal to the Congress. 311p. Supt. of Docs. Washington 25, D.C. '55.

United States. House of Representatives. Committee on Banking and Currency. Slum clearance and urban renewal; report no 1 of the subcommittee on housing. 84th Congress, 2d session. 33p. Supt. of Docs. Washington 25, D.C. '56.

*United States. House of Representatives. Committee on Government Operations. Creation of a Department of Urbiculture; hearings, July 26, 1955, before a subcommittee, on HR 1864. 52p. 84th Congress, 1st session. The Committee. Washington 25, D.C.
    Reprinted in this book: Statement by Representative J. Arthur Younger. p2-4.

United States. Housing and Home Finance Agency. How localities can develop a workable program for urban renewal. 12p. Supt. of Docs. Washington 25, D.C. '55.

United States. Housing and Home Finance Agency. Introduction to urban renewal. 12p. Supt. of Docs. Washington 25, D.C. '54.

United States. Housing and Home Finance Agency. Slums and blight: disease of urban life. (Urban renewal bulletin no2) 22p. Supt. of Docs. Washington 25, D.C. '56.

United States. Housing and Home Finance Agency. Urban renewal: what it is. 11p. Supt. of Docs. Washington 25, D.C. '55.

United States. Housing and Home Finance Agency. Workable program. 8p. Supt. of Docs. Washington 25, D.C. '55.

University of California. Department of City and Regional Planning. Problems of decentralization and metropolitan areas. 46p. mimeo. The University. Berkeley, Calif. '54.

Walker, R. A. Planning function in urban government. 410p. University of Chicago Press. Chicago. '50.

Warren, R. L. Studying your community. 325p. Russell Sage Foundation. New York. '55.

Woodbury, Coleman and others. Future of cities and urban redevelopment. 764p. University of Chicago Press. Chicago. '53.

Woodbury, Coleman and others. Urban redevelopment problems and practices. 525p. University of Chicago Press. Chicago. '53.

PERIODICALS

American Builder. 74:107-11. S. '52. Park Forest shopping center proves value of good planning.

American Builder. 76:284-5. Ja. '54. Best answer to rehabilitation is awakened community pride.

American Builder. 76:125-8. F. '54. Land planning is worth it. U. A. Denker.

American Builder. 76:232-4. Ag. '54. High points in the development of land planning. M. S. Wehrly.

American Business. 23:26-7+. Mr. '53. When big business comes to a country town. John Garth.

*American City. 69:103-4. O. '54. How a small city benefits from planning. L. R. Cooper.
  Each issue of this periodical has many articles concerning community planning. See the subject index in each issue.

American Journal of Public Health. 45:1-10. Ja. '55. Suburbanization and suburbia. Coleman Woodbury.

American Journal of Sociology. 60:471-86. Mr. '55. Urbanism in the United States. D. J. Bogue.

American Magazine. 159:55. Mr. '55. Rx for tired towns.

American Mercury. 81:67-70. S. '55. Surprises in the suburbs. E. C. Hanford.

*American Scholar. 23:341-52. Summer '54. Rebuilding American cities: the challenge of urban redevelopment. N. S. Keith.

American Water Works Association Journal. 47:945-72. O. '55. Extension of public services to suburban areas; panel discussion.

Annals of the American Academy of Political and Social Science. 243:1-162. N. '45. Building the future city. R. B. Mitchell and others.

Annals of the American Academy of Political and Social Science. 302:8-16. N. '55. City planning process: a framework for community education. Francis Violich.

Architectural Forum. 100:128-9. Ap. '54. Chicago devises a plan to crack the slum collar around its Loop.

Architectural Forum. 100:152-9. Je. '54. Sacramento, a model for small city redevelopment.

Architectural Forum. 101:128-47. Jl.; 120-7. Ag.; 158-61. O. '54. Industry builds Kitimat, first complete new town in North America.

Architectural Forum. 101:140-3. S. '54. Inside Philadelphia; a new kind of new town, Eastwick.

Architectural Forum. 102:122-31+. Je. '55. How to rebuild cities downtown; roundtable report.

Architectural Forum. 103:130-9. Ag. '55. Cleveland, city with a deadline.

Architectural Record. 115:170-7. My. '54. Cities not for dying; redevelopment boom.

Atlanta Economic Review. 4:1-5+. O. '54. Economic development and city planning.

Banking. 47:54-5. My. '55. Housing blight in the midst of boom. F. A. Irving.

Better Homes and Gardens. 33:42+. O. '55. Is your neighborhood ready for action. Henry Lee.

Bulletin of the Atomic Scientists. 9:265-7. S. '53. City planning in Project East River. Donald Monson.

*Bulletin of the Atomic Scientists. 9:268. S. '53. Defense considerations in city planning; statement by the American Institute of Planners.

Burroughs Clearing House. 39:33-5+. Ag. '55. Development corporations. Ed Tyng.

Business Week. p70-2+. Ap. 11, '53. Pittsburgh's answer to the high cost of squalor.

Business Week. p76-8+. My. 30, '53. Cave city: Arkansas makes its own revolution.

Business Week. p72-3+. My. 30, '53. Ham Moses: only way out is to grow.

Business Week. p 146. Jl. 18, '53. Suburbia; its taxes ache.

Business Week. p 148+. Jl. 18, '53. Fringe areas in California.

Business Week. p 103-4+. N. 21, '53. Land grab, Texas style.

Business Week. p 106+. My. 1, '54. Fringe trouble ending, and just beginning.

Business Week. p68+. Je. 12, '54. Suburbs grow while New York rests.

*Business Week. p42-4+. Ja. 15, '55. Retailers' problem: reviving a sick old "Downtown."

*Business Week. p64-6+. Ja. 22, '55. City-suburb federation: how good an answer is it? Toronto experiment.
     Reply. p 15. F. 26, '55.
Business Week. p 142-4. Jl. 9, '55. Reviving the city.

Business Week. p 130-2+. S. 10, '55. New St. Louis rips up its past.

Changing Times. 9:28-30. Ap. '55. Our expensive slums.

*Changing Times. 9:21-4. S. '55. Trouble with your town is . . .

Christian Century. 73:170-2. F. 8, '56. San Francisco Bay area. Mel Scott.

Civil Engineering. 22:685-8. S. '52. Our expanding cities depend on good planning. L. V. Sheridan.

*Collier's. 130:34-7. N. 1, '52. Solving that parking problem. C. T. McGavin with S. V. Jones.

Collier's. 133:48-50+. Ap. 30, '54. How your town can avoid a recession. W. L. Batt, Jr. and Ronald Scheller.

*Commentary. 17:75-82. Ja. '54. Where city planning stands today. Frank Fisher.

Commercial and Financial Chronicle. 176:2131. D. 4, '52. Impact on city property values resulting from decentralization. W. L. C. Wheaton.

Commonweal. 61:647-50. Mr. 25, '55. Sin of slums. John Stanley.

Electrical World. 145:76-82. Ja. 9, '56. Why Action?

Engineering News Record. 150:49-50+. My. 28, '53. Baltimore plan: is this the way to beat slums.

Engineering News Record. 151:49-50+. Ag. 13, '53. Columbus stresses planning to insure capital's future.

Engineering News Record. 152:61-2. Ja. 7, '54. City needs inventoried: $287-million plan results: Louisville, Ky.

Engineering News Record. 152:181+. F. 18, '54. Cities decentralizing; maybe not.

Engineering News Record. 152:33-4. Mr. 25, '54. Chicago unfolds big development plan.

Federal Reserve Bank of Chicago Business Conditions. p 10-15. N. '54. The big city: are its days numbered.

Food for Thought. 16:26-30. S.-O. '55. Is this community planning. M. G. Ross.

Fortune. 47:112-17+. My.; 126-31+. Je.; 48:84-9+. Jl.; 120-2+. Ag. '53. Transients [of Suburbia]. W. H. Whyte, Jr.

Fortune. 48:128-31+. N. '53. Lush new suburban market.

Fortune. 48:231. N. '53. Who are the suburbanites?

*Fortune. 51:116-26+. Je. '55. Battle for Chicago. Daniel Seligman.

Harper's Magazine. 207:25-32. N.; 80-6. D. '53. Mass-produced suburbs. Harry Henderson.

Harper's Magazine. 208:21-8. Je.; 209:47-53. Jl. '54. Big change in suburbia. F. L. Allen.

Harper's Magazine. 212:10-12+. Ja. '56. Beating the Bali Ha'i racket. Bernard De Voto.

Harper's Magazine. 212:76-9. Mr. '56. St. Louis wakes itself up. Avis Carlson.

Horizons for Modern Pennsylvania Local Government. 1:1-2+. Time to attack metropolitan confusion.

House and Home. 3:44-5. Ja. '53. Fight against slums.

House and Home. 4:130-5. O. '53. How U. S. cities are meeting the challenge of rehabilitation.

House and Home. 5:170+. F. '54. Will urban rehabilitation lead to demand for political overhaul of city governments. R. E. Merrian.

House and Home. 5:66+. My. '54. How U. S. cities are growing.

House and Home. 6:100-133. O. '54. Housing Act of 1954.

Journal of the American Institute of Planners. 19:3-9. Winter '53. Planning and political participation. H. J. Gans.

Journal of the American Institute of Planners. 19:95-102. Spring '53. Rethinking urban redevelopment. R. L. Creighton.

Journal of the American Institute of Planners. 19:147-50. Summer '53. Planner's relationship with the city manager. W. I. Goodman.

Journal of the American Institute of Planners. 20:21-5. Winter '54. Chicago redevelopment. I. J. Back.

*Journal of the American Institute of Planners. 20:189-91. Fall '54. Planning in a free society. H. S. Churchill.

Journal of the American Institute of Planners. 21:62-6. Spring-Summer '55. Planner in a democratic society—a credo. J. T. Howard.

Land Economics. 28:341-52. N. '52. Urban size: an assessment. R. M. Lillibridge.

Land Economics. 30:320-8. N. '54. City planning, administration, and politics. C. S. Ascher.

Land Economics. 31:275-80. Ag. '55. Industrial decentralization as a factor in rural-urban fringe development. L. G. Reeder.

Land Economics. 31:280-2. Ag. '55. Urban intent and urban expansion. J. D. Fellmann.

Law and Contemporary Problems. 20:351-529. Summer '55. Urban housing and planning. C. M. Haar and others.

Library Journal. 80:2195-200. O. 15, '55. Community development. H. C. Mial.

Look. 17:42-6+. F. 10, '53; 18:51-7+. F. 9, '54; 19:73-5+, F. 8, '55. All-American cities, National municipal league and Look citations.

Mademoiselle. 41:102-3+. My. '55. Habitat exurbia. A. C. Spectorsky.

Management Review. 41:572-6. S. '52. Municipalities and industrial location. J. D. Garwood.

*Manufacturers Record. 123:52-3+. D. '54. Arkansas reaping benefits from Ham Moses' big plan.

Minnesota Municipalities. 39:205-9. Ag. '54. City planning implications of industrial location. F. A. Pitkin.

Municipal Finance. 27:15-20. Ag. '54. Some observations on regional planning. George Gathercole.

National Council Outlook. 5:9+. My. '55. Spiritual focus for the neighborhood.

National Municipal Review. 43:440. S. '54. Model planning law progressing rapidly.

National Municipal Review. 43:549-52. N. '54. Time to attack metropolitan confusion.

National Municipal Review. 44:82-8. F. '55. Cities step over line. R. W. Maddox.

National Municipal Review. 44:466-8+. O. '55. Detroit's regional plan. T. L. Blakeman.

*Nation's Business. 41:32-3. Je. '53. Mass transportation or mess? Sam Stavisky.

Nation's Business. 41:84-9. N. '53. Let the people lead the town. M. M. Hunt.

Nation's Business. 42:101-2. Je. '54. Plans for growth: Hollywood, Fla.

Nation's Business. 42:93. Jl. '54. Wanted: city planners.

Nation's Business. 43:46+. My. '55. Local tax jumps city limits. C. W. Magrue.

New Jersey Municipalities. 30:7-10. N. '55. Importance of new planning legislation to your community. H. H. Smith.

New York Times. p93. Ja. 3, '56. Stores again eye downtown trade.

New York Times Magazine. p 14+. S. 19, '54. Homogenized children of new suburbia. S. M. Gruenberg.
> Discussion. p4. O. 10, '54.
> Abridged. Practical Home Economics. 34:24+. S. '55.

*New York Times Magazine. p 14+. Ap. 24, '55. States eclipse the cities. T. C. Desmond.
> Reply. D. H. Hepburn. p4. My. 8, '55.
> Abridged. American City. 70:19. Je. '55.

New York Times Magazine. p 14+. Mr. 6, '55. All suburbia is divided into three parts. C. H. Palmer.

New York Times Magazine. p 17+. My. 15, '55. From the suburbs back to the city. Herbert Mitgang.
> Discussion. p4. My. 29, '55.

*New York Times Magazine. p26-7+. S. 25, '55. Rebirth of a community. Gertrude Samuels.

*New York Times Magazine. p 13+. Ja. 8, '56. Moses recipe for better parks. Robert Moses.

*New York Times Magazine. p26-7+. Ja. 29, '56. New way of life in Britain's New Towns. Albert Mayer.

New Yorker. 31:115+. Mr. 19; 97+. Ap. 2; 78+. Ap. 16; 166+. Je. 11, '55. Roaring traffic's boom. Lewis Mumford.

Newsweek. 43:74-5. Mr. 29, '54. New hearts for our cities.

*Parent's Magazine. 31:54+. Mr. '56. It's time for ACTION. F. A. Irving.

Proceedings of the American Society of Civil Engineers. 79 [no 194]: 1-8. Je. '53. City planning techniques. R. H. Riley.

Proceedings of the American Society of Civil Engineers. 79 [no285]:1-7. S. '53. Community and neighborhood development. R. H. Riley.

Proceedings of the American Society of Civil Engineers. 81 [no600]:1-6. Ja. '55. Denver's master street plan. J. S. Marshall.

Proceedings of the American Society of Civil Engineers. 81 [no601]:1-14. Ja. '55. Pittsburgh's comprehensive improvement program. P. H. Martin.

Proceedings of the American Society of Civil Engineers. 81 [no602]:1-8. Ja. '55. Organization for metropolitan traffic and transportation planning. C. A. Blessing.

Proceedings of the American Society of Civil Engineers. 81 [no769]:1-7. Ag. '55. Urban transportation problem. H. E. Davis.

Proceedings of the American Society of Civil Engineers. 81 [no785]:1-8. Ag. '55. Urban renewal and the rebuilding of American cities. J. W. Follen.

Proceedings of the American Society of Civil Engineers. 81 [no832]:1-6. N. '55. Impact of atomic development on growth and planning of urban regions. P. H. Martin.

Proceedings of the American Society of Civil Engineers. 81 [no834]:1-9. Nov. '55. Planning new cities. Albert Mayer.

Planning and Civic Comment. 20:1-5. D. '54. New view of planning the metropolis. F. C. Moore.

Public Administration Review. 14:85-95. Spring '54. Metropolitan government in Toronto. W. W. Crouch.

Public Management. 25:150-3. Jl. '53. Future of the central business district. J. D. Carroll, Jr.

*Public Management. 35:271-5. D. '53. Trends and forecasts in fringe areas. J. C. Bollens.
    Same. American City. 68:122-4. D. '53.

Public Management. 36:192-4. My. '54. Are suburbs parasites? J. L. Scott.

Public Management. 36:126-9. Je. '54. Cities and the urban fringe. J. C. Bollens.

Public Management. 37:11-13. Ja. '55. Trends and forecasts in planning. H. K. Menhinick.

*Public Management. 37:74-7. Ap. '55. Urban renewal—a program for cities. W. L. Slayton.

Public Management. 37:252-4. N. '55. Trends in planning. Dennis O'Harrow.

Public Works. 84:61-2+. Mr. '53. Problems of subdivision, zoning and private streets: Princeton, N.J. J. R. Riker.

*Public Works. 85:134-5. Mr. '54. Controlling regional development. J. F. Base.

*Reader's Digest. 67:87-90. N. '55. Slum clearance pays extra dividends. Donald Robinson.
    Same expanded with title Slum clearance pays off. National Municipal Review. 44:461-5. O. '55.

Recreation. 47:80-2. F.; 152-5. Mr.; 214-17. Ap.; 276-9. My. '54. Planning for recreation in the modern city. H. R. Pomeroy and others.

Reporter. 11:35-6+. N. 18, '54. Let's plan our cities before it's too late. Albert Mayer.

*Reporter. 13:14-18. S. 8, '55. How long will New York wait? A. A. Berle, Jr.

Rural Sociology. 18:101-20. Je. '53. Rural-urban fringe. S. A. Queen and others.

Sales Management. 76:84-103. N. 10, '55. Trends in metro areas, 1945-55.

Saturday Evening Post. 226:30+. Ag. 8, '53. They said no to progress. J. A. Morris.

Saturday Evening Post. 226:22-3+. Je. 5; 38-9+. Je. 12; 30+, Je. 19, '54. Downtown isn't damned. Hal Burton.

*Saturday Evening Post. 228:19-21+. S. 17; 32-3+. S. 24; 30+. O. 1, '55. Trouble in the suburbs. Hal Burton.
    Reprinted in this book. Part 1.
    Discussion. 228:4+. O. 29, '55.

Saturday Review. 38:10-13. My. 21, '55. Future of the city. F. L. Wright.

Science Digest. 37:31. Je. '55. Americans are mainly city dwellers.

Scientific American. 190:54-63. Ap. '54. Form of cities. Kevin Lynch.

Scientific Monthly. 81:38-41. Jl. '55. City neighborhood and village.

Senior Scholastic. 64:11-12+. Ap. 28, '54. American cities on the move.

*Senior Scholastic. 67:11-12. O. 20, '55. Our mushrooming cities.

Southwestern Social Science Quarterly. 35:235-43. D. '54. Extraterritorial jurisdiction as an approach to suburban problems of small cities. R. T. Daland.

State Government. 27:203-4+. O. '54. States and urban renewal. W. L. Slayton.

State Government. 28:259-61. N. '55. American Council to Improve Our Neighborhoods. K. H. Stone.

*Steel. 133:66-7. S. 14, '53. Area development puts the welcome mat out for industry.

Steel. 134:73-4. Mr. 8, '54. Reversing the jobless trend by your own bootstraps.

Technology Review. 56:201-4+. F. '54. Today's challenge to the family in suburbia. K. T. Compton.

Time. 63:102. Mr. 22, '54. Flight to the suburbs.

Time. 66:25-8. D. 5, '55. Rebirth of the cities.

United States News & World Report. 39:44-7. N. 25, '55. Rush to the suburbs.

*United States News & World Report. 40:37-40. Mr. 2, '56. Rush to suburbs just starting.

Urban Land. 12:1+. Mr. '53. Redevelopment restated.

Urban Land. 12:1+. S. '53. Trends for modern communities. M. S. Wehrly.

Urban Land. 12:1+. O. '53. Apropos—any city. R. C. Bond.

Western City. 30:42-7. Mr. '54. Lakewood story. A. G. Will.

Western City. 30:29-30. Ag. '54. Planning as insurance to avoid past errors and project future city needs.

Western City. 30:44-5+. S. '54. Cities and the urban fringe. J. C. Bollens.

Western City. 31:35-6. Ag. '55. Story of China Lake, federal community. R. C. O'Reilly.

*Western City. 31:56+. Ag. '55. Some political and administrative considerations in urban planning. E. A. Engelbert and J. H. Walters.

Vital Speeches of the Day. 21:1497-1503. S. 15, '55. Metropolitan quandary. C. A. Harrell.

15751